Gizmos & Gadgets

WILLIAMSON
KIDS CAN!

Dedication

To my son, Zev, whose boundless imagination propels him
so joyfully into the universe of gizmos and inventions.

✹

Acknowledgments

My deep gratitude to Melvin Frankel for his expert review and
tireless help in doing justice to the many facets of physics
encountered in writing this book.

Thanks to innovative Boulder Creek teacher Kathryn Tilzey for
sharing her invention resource trove.

To Savlan Hauser, my appreciation for the original cover sketches.

✹

Other Williamson Publishing Books by Jill Frankel Hauser:

KIDS' CRAZY ART CONCOCTIONS
50 Mysterious Mixtures for Art & Craft Fun

SUPER SCIENCE CONCOCTIONS
50 Mysterious Mixtures for Fabulous Fun

SCIENCE PLAY!
Beginning Discoveries for 2- to 6-Year-Olds

GROWING UP READING
Learning to Read Through Creative Play

Copyright © 1999 by Jill Frankel Hauser

Kids Can!®, **Little Hands**®, and **Tales Alive!**® are registered trademarks of Williamson Publishing Company. **Kaleidoscope Kids**™ and **Good Times!**™ are trademarks of Williamson Publishing.

Library of Congress
Cataloging-in-Publication Data

Hauser, Jill Frankel, 1950-
  Gizmos & gadgets: creating science contraptions that work (and knowing why) / by Jill Frankel Hauser.
    p. cm.
  "Williamson kids can! book."
  Includes index.
  Summary: Provides instructions for making 75 contraptions that demonstrate friction, gravity, energy, motion, and other principles of physics and explains how to think like an inventor.
  ISBN 1-885593-26-0 (alk. paper)
  1. Discoveries in science — Juvenile literature.
  2. Inventions — Juvenile literature. 3. Creativity in science — Juvenile literature.
  [1. Inventions. 2. Physics — Experiments.
  3. Experiments. 4. Scientific recreations.] I. Title.
Q180.55.D57H34   1999
                                  98–30302
500 — dc21
                        CIP
                        AC

Kids Can! ® Series Editor: **Susan Williamson**
Illustrations: **Michael Kline Illustration**
Book design: **Joseph Lee Design: Kristin DiVona,**
                        Joseph Lee
Cover design: **Trezzo-Braren Studio**
Printing: **Capital City Press**

Williamson Publishing Co.
P.O. Box 185
Charlotte, Vermont 05445
1-800-234-8791

Manufactured in the United States of America

10 9 8 7 6 5 4 3 2

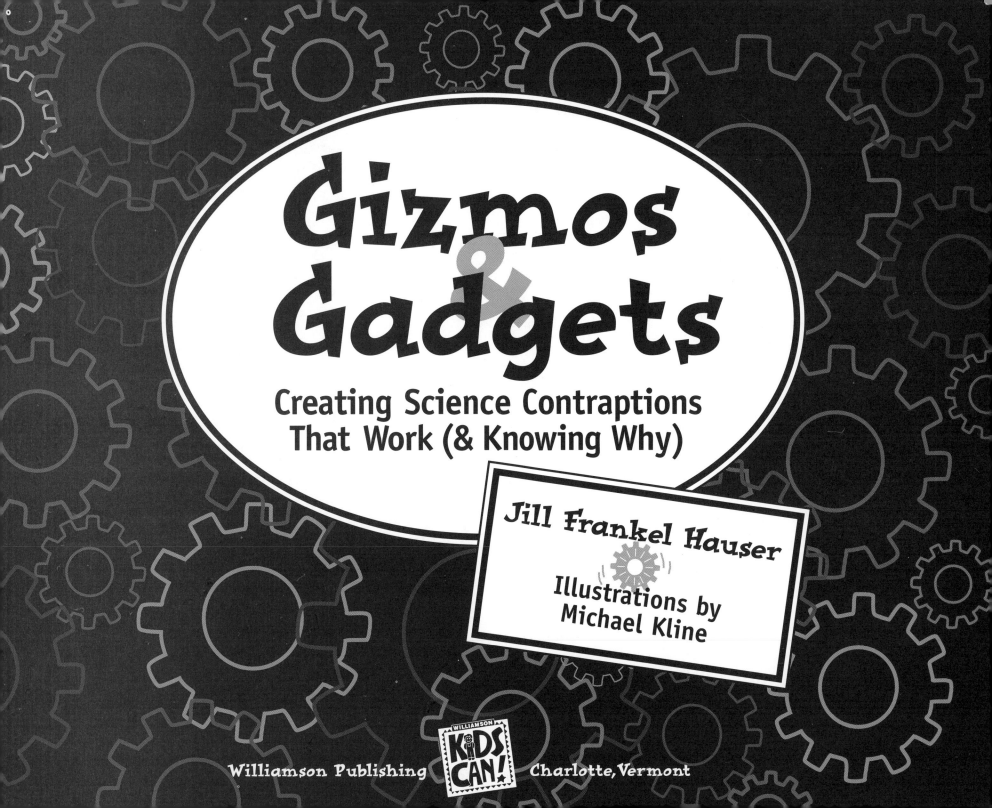

Gizmos & Gadgets

Creating Science Contraptions That Work (& Knowing Why)

Jill Frankel Hauser

Illustrations by
Michael Kline

Williamson Publishing   Charlotte, Vermont

Contents

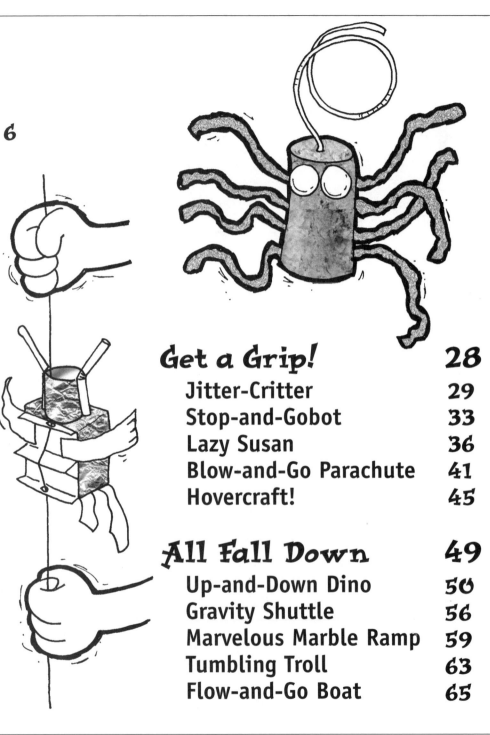

Welcome to the World of Gizmos!

Want to build a catapult that sends marshmallows flying? Or how about making a toy bird that balances on your finger, while resting on the tip of its beak? Maybe you'd like to build a contraption that travels on an invisible cushion of air. Or would you like to create your *own* awesome gadget?

Well, you can start constructing now! Ingenious gizmos and cool contraptions are just waiting to be made from materials found around your home and school. Build gizmos that spin, glide, wobble, and whiz. Create contraptions that fling, swing, and collide. It's easy — and fun! — to explore the amazing, action-packed world of motion. Just s-t-r-e-t-c-h your imagination, gather a few supplies, and then, let's get started.

Power a merry-go-round with the stored energy in a rubber band?
Use the force of friction to operate a "gobot"?
Activate the mighty head of a dino with the force of gravity?

Miraculous, you say? Not at all. There's nothing magical about these contraptions once you *understand* what makes them work. And that's true of just about everything. Understanding opens all kinds of doors, because then you can *apply what you know to new situations*. Inventors do it all the time! And so can you. The contraptions in this book are perfect springboards for your own awesome creations and inventions that will astound and amaze just about everyone!

Gathering Gizmo Supplies

The contraptions in this book are made from safe, inexpensive, easy-to-find materials. Many are simply old items you can recycle into exciting creations. Scrounge around and see what interesting stuff you can come up with. Here's a list of some of the items you'll want to keep on hand:

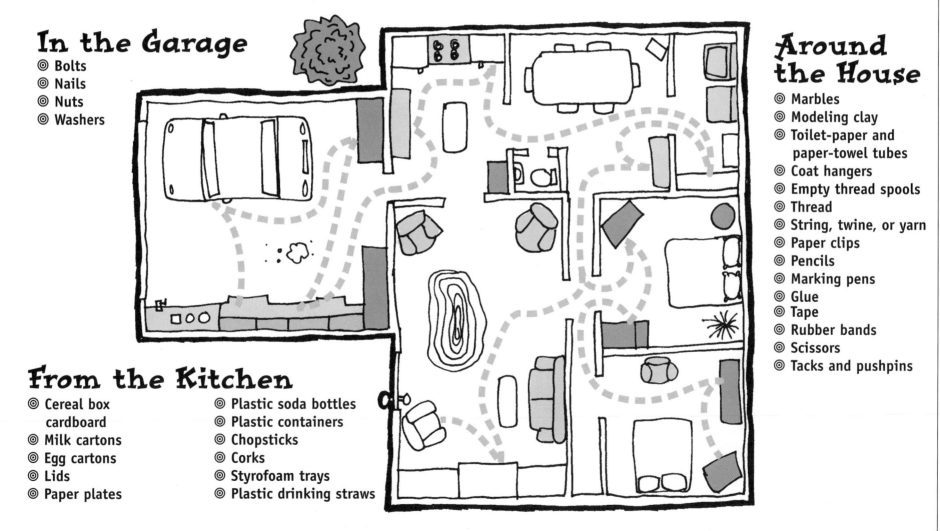

In the Garage
- Bolts
- Nails
- Nuts
- Washers

From the Kitchen
- Cereal box cardboard
- Milk cartons
- Egg cartons
- Lids
- Paper plates
- Plastic soda bottles
- Plastic containers
- Chopsticks
- Corks
- Styrofoam trays
- Plastic drinking straws

Around the House
- Marbles
- Modeling clay
- Toilet-paper and paper-towel tubes
- Coat hangers
- Empty thread spools
- Thread
- String, twine, or yarn
- Paper clips
- Pencils
- Marking pens
- Glue
- Tape
- Rubber bands
- Scissors
- Tacks and pushpins

Motion Commotion

Hold everything! Stand still. How long can you keep that pose? It's hard, isn't it? Motion is so much a part of our lives that we hardly know it's there ... until we have to stop, that is! All day long, we're moving from here to there.

Can you believe there are rules, called *scientific laws*, to explain all motion? Although you're just thinking about fun when you shoot a marble or dive into a pool, you can't make a move that goes against the rules of science. As you make these gizmos that cause a commotion, you'll discover the laws of motion!

Where's the motion? Look around. Cars, airplanes, and trucks are big movers, but what else can you spot that's on the go? There's you and the trillions of other living creatures! What about leaves swaying in the breeze? A fly creeping across the wall? A second hand ticking? You turning the pages of this book?

Inertia Zoom Ball

Find a friend to play inertia zoom ball. Each player holds onto two handles and moves away from the other player until the strings are tight. Slide the zoom ball to one end. If you are the player closest to the zoom ball, snap your hands apart to send the zoom ball to your friend. To receive the zoom ball, keep your hands together.

Tools & Supplies

◎ Scissors
◎ Two 1-quart (1-L) plastic soda bottles
◎ Masking tape
◎ Colored construction paper and contrasting ribbons (optional)
◎ Two 12-foot (2.4-m) strings
◎ Two plastic-ring six-pack holders

Let's build it!

1. With a grown-up's help, cut the bottoms from two soda bottles. Tape the bottles end to end so they form a football shape. Cover them with a sleeve of colored paper, if desired, and wrap a contrasting colorful ribbon in a spiral pattern over the sleeve. Tape in place.

2. Thread the two strings through the necks.
3. Cut the six-pack holder rings apart to form four two-loop handles. Tie a set of handles to the ends of each string. Now, zoom!

Be Pushy

How'd That Happen?

Yank the strings outward and the zoom ball goes flying. Why? The pushing action of the strings sets it in motion. When the zoom ball reaches the other end of the strings, an opposite pushing action (your friend's string-snapping motion) stops the ball for a moment and then sends it flying in the reverse direction.

PAPER CLIP

CORK

THUMBTACKS

PIPE CLEANERS

It's the Law...
The First Law of Motion!

Congratulations! You've just demonstrated the first law of motion, also called the *law of inertia* (in-ER-shuh). It states that **without a force like a push or pull, an object won't budge. And once it's going, it won't stop moving in a straight line unless it's forced to change its movement by another push or a pull.** You and your friend have overcome the zoom ball's *inertia* (how boring) with your *forceful* tugs (how moving)!

Keep on doin' what you're doin'. Do you ever feel as if you've got inertia when your alarm goes off in the morning? How about when you're running a race or working on your favorite gizmo? You just don't want to change what you're already doing!

Whose Bright Idea?

ISAAC NEWTON

Presenting Sir Isaac Newton!

Have you ever wondered about motion? Well, Sir Isaac Newton sure did. He came up with three simple laws that explain the fantastic process of moving from here to there. And you've just figured out the first one! Look for clues to the others as you make more gizmos.

Newton's questioning mind made him one of the greatest scientists of all time. He looked for answers to what seemed like simple questions. When he was 23 and a student at Cambridge University in England, the school was closed because of the plague. But Newton's mind remained open. He studied on his own at his mother's farm. There, he made amazing discoveries we still rely on today.

During his lifetime, Newton described the laws of motion, solved mysteries of color and light, explained how gravity keeps the planets orbiting around the sun, and invented calculus (a kind of math) to explain his discoveries. His questioning mind helped him find the answers!

Fast Physics

Lazy Pencils

Place round pencils in a drawer so that their long sides are against the front of the drawer. Open the drawer quickly. What happens to the pencils? Can you figure out why?

P.S. You'll find answers to questions like these at the bottom of the page, throughout the book.

!? Imagine a force so powerful it can overcome the inertia of a critter at rest, causing it to leap more than 130 times its own height! It's flea power! A flea's mighty muscles send it soaring 8 inches (20 cm) upward — and right onto Rover!

Science Speak!

All matter (see page 51) — a rock, a house, even you — has *inertia*. It does whatever it's already doing, whether it's in motion or still, unless it's *forced* to change. Some sort of force, either a push or a pull, is needed to

• *set an object in motion*
• *make a moving object change direction*
• *make a moving object move faster*
• *make a moving object come to screeching stop!*

What pushes you into action? You may think it's that sweet voice in the kitchen asking you to set the table, but actually it's the force of your muscles!

Answer: *The pencils are at rest. When the drawer moves underneath them, they try to stay put (inertia at work), which makes them end up in the back of the drawer.*

Set a small doll on top of a toy car. Set up a heavy block (no higher than the car) a few feet away. Now, push the car into the block. *Crash!* What happens to the car and the doll? Using Newton's first law of motion, figure out why.

You know that an object in motion stays in motion unless stopped by a force. A force (the block) stopped the car, but not the doll. It stayed in motion ... until gravity (see page 49) forced it to bonk its head on the pavement! Seat belts, anyone?

It's Magic ... Inertia Coin Magic!

These coins may seem to behave in strange ways, but they're just following the laws of the universe! Challenge your friends to predict what they think will happen when you explain what you plan to do. Then, amaze them with your tricks.

Tower Power
Make a tower of nickels. Try to knock it down, one nickel at a time, by using the tower's inertia. Flick a nickel sharply at the bottom coin. What happens?

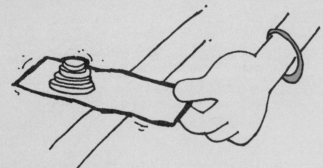

Money Pyramid
Stack a nickel, penny, and dime by size, largest to smallest, on a quarter base. Set the pyramid on a strip of paper that hangs over a table edge. Hold onto the end of the strip and quickly snap the paper away. What happens to the pyramid? Where is the inertia advantage in your magic?

Independent Penny
Set an index card or paper over the mouth of a bottle. Set a penny on the card directly over the mouth. Flick the card with your finger. Where does the penny go?

Force Fun

What makes these gizmos move? You do! They won't change course without a force … a flick that makes them fly.

Flick with greater force, and what happens to each gizmo? You're on the trail to figuring out Newton's second law of motion. Make the Dart Launcher on page 14 for more clues.

Sailing Streamer

Cut three strips of newspaper, each about 2 ¹/₂ inches (6 cm) wide. Tape them end to end on both sides of the paper. Rub each side of the streamer with the side of a crayon to make the paper slick and give it color. Tape the edge of the streamer to a chopstick. Tightly wind up the streamer and hold it in place with a rubber band. Leave the streamer wound up overnight.

To play: Remove the rubber band and flick the tip of the chopstick out and then back. What happens to the streamer?

Flick Ball

Fold a sheet of paper in half the long way. Fold up a triangle at one end. Keep folding triangles over each other, tucking the end flap into the "pocket" of the last triangle.

To play: You and a friend sit on either side of a table. Use your finger and thumb to flick the gizmo back and forth. Or, take turns making goals, flicking the triangle from one end of the table to the other. If the Flick Ball balances over the edge of the table, it's a goal.

Dart Launcher

Which do you predict will move a dart farther — your arm or a launcher?
A launcher pulled back all the way or partway? Experiment to find out.

Tools & Supplies
◎ Paper
◎ Stapler
◎ Rubber band
◎ Pencil or chopstick

Let's build it!

1. Using a full sheet of paper for the larger dart and a quarter sheet of paper for the smaller dart, make two darts following the folds shown.

2. Set the keel (the bottom fold) of the smaller dart into the groove of the large dart. Their noses should be even, with the small dart tipping upward. Staple through the keel to hold this position.

3. Fold a piece (about an eighth of a sheet) of paper in half vertically. Staple it on to the keel of the larger dart, to create a hook for the launcher.

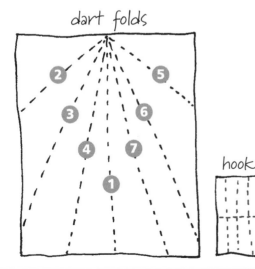

dart folds

hook

small dart

large dart

keel

4. To make the launcher, loop a rubber band around a pencil or chopstick. Then loop the free end of the rubber band around the hook under the keel of the larger dart.

5. Pull back while pinching the rubber band and the keel. Aim the dart above the launcher. Release.

FORCE ON COURSE

How'd That Happen?

Your dart went from resting to soaring, thanks to the force from your muscles or the force of the launcher. But which way made the dart fly faster and travel farther? The greater force made a greater change in motion. (Does that sound like a law? You bet it does!)

Part 1 — It's the Law...
The Second Law of Motion!

Take a bow: You've just demonstrated Newton's second law of motion! It states that **the greater the force on an object, the greater the change in motion.**

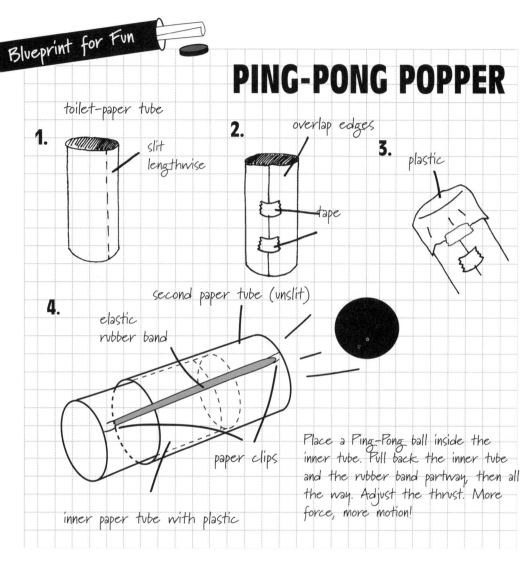

Blueprint for Fun

PING-PONG POPPER

toilet-paper tube

1. slit lengthwise

2. overlap edges / tape

3. plastic

4.
elastic rubber band
second paper tube (unslit)
paper clips
inner paper tube with plastic

Place a Ping-Pong ball inside the inner tube. Pull back the inner tube and the rubber band partway, then all the way. Adjust the thrust. More force, more motion!

Science Clues

Make a catapult that uses the second law of motion to get marshmallows moving! See page 120.

Mark and Sammy Know!
(Mark McGwire and Sammy Sosa, that is!)

!? Why didn't Mark McGwire's record-breaking home-run ball fly on forever?

Grab a softball and a bat, and head outside. Set the ball on the ground. What happens? Nothing, of course. The ball has inertia and won't budge until you pick it up and throw it with your muscle power (Newton's first law). Try again, but this time use the bat to give the ball a mighty whack. Watch that ball travel faster and farther, following Newton's second law of motion!

Fast Physics
Eraser-Paper Race

Set an eraser next to a crumpled quarter sheet of paper on a smooth tabletop. Which one travels farther if you flick it gently with your finger? Which one has more mass (weight)?

!? ◎ Imagine yourself as the goalie in a soccer game. Two balls are coming toward you, one traveling really fast and the other very slowly. Which would you rather stop?
◎ They're coming at you — and fast! Which would you rather stop: a Ping-Pong ball or a bowling ball?

318

451

Answers: *The slow ball has less force so it is easier to stop. The Ping-Pong ball has less mass so it will require the least force to change its motion. Mark McGwire's home-run ball didn't have enough force to overcome gravity and friction. **Eraser-Paper Race:** When adding equal force (flicks), the object with less mass moves farther.*

It's the Law...
The Second Law of Motion! 2 PART

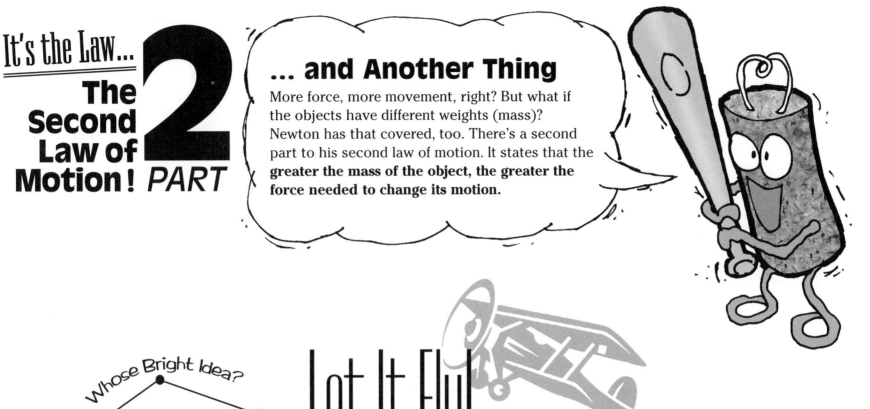

... and Another Thing

More force, more movement, right? But what if the objects have different weights (mass)? Newton has that covered, too. There's a second part to his second law of motion. It states that the **greater the mass of the object, the greater the force needed to change its motion.**

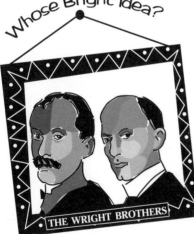

Whose Bright Idea?

THE WRIGHT BROTHERS

Let It Fly!

It all started with a gadget their dad brought home. A tiny helicopter propelled by a rubber band was the perfect toy for the Wright boys, Wilbur and Orville. "If we could just make it larger, it could carry people," they thought. Although their scheme failed, they were now inventors! It took lots of experimenting, first with kites and then with gliders, to invent their dream flying machine.

Once they mastered the ups, downs, and turns of flying, the next challenge was how to power the contraption. Could they find an engine that was lightweight, yet powerful enough to get the plane into the air?

As great inventors, the brothers were problem solvers. Along with Charles Taylor, they built just such an engine and propeller themselves. It worked! On December 17, 1903, their 12-second flight was long enough to prove that a heavier-than-air contraption could actually fly! Can you imagine their excitement?

Action-Reaction Rocket

Three … two … one … blast off! Discover Sir Isaac Newton's third law of motion by making a rocket that will shoot across your living room.

Tools & Supplies
◎ Tape
◎ Plastic drinking straw
◎ Plastic bag, about the shape of the inflated balloon — a bread bag works well
◎ Paper or plastic streamers
◎ String, 25 feet (7.5 m)
◎ Long, tube-shaped balloons

straw

plastic bag

Science Speak!

What's the *action*? It's the force — a push or a pull — on an object. A *reaction* is the equal push or pull of the object in the opposite direction.

Let's build it!

1. Tape a drinking straw along the top edge of a plastic bag. Tape paper streamers to the bottom edge of the bag's opening.

2. Thread about 25 feet (7.5 m) of string through the straw. Tie each end of string to the back of a different chair; then, set the chairs apart so that the string is taut. Set the bag at one end of the string, with the open end closest to the chair.

3. Blow up a tube-shaped balloon and set it in the bag, holding tight to the balloon's neck. When you're ready, count down to zero, and let go of the neck of the balloon. What do you observe?

IT'S A BLAST!

How'd That Happen?

W hen you let go of the neck of the balloon rocket, the balloon blasts forward as the air rushes out the opposite end, forcing your plastic-bag rocket down the string. One **action** (air rushing out) produces an opposite **reaction** (the balloon shooting off in the other direction).

ACTION ← → REACTION

Fast Physics

Reaction Action

Grab your skates and a friend for a little physics fun. Face your friend, palms together. Ready to roll? Push gently on your friend's hands and you'd expect your friend to roll away. But what really happens?

It's the Law...

Newton's Third Law of Motion!

Hip, hip, hooray! You've just demonstrated Newton's third law of motion! It states that **for every action, there is an equal but opposite reaction.**

Answer: You both roll backward! Action, reaction in action!

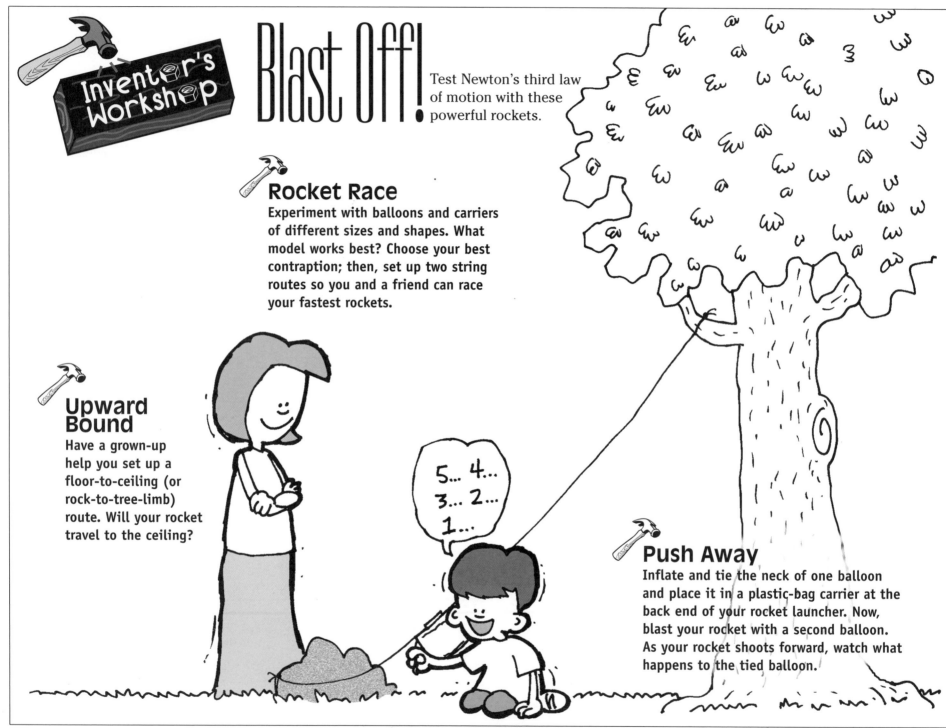

Inventor's Workshop

Blast Off!

Test Newton's third law of motion with these powerful rockets.

Rocket Race

Experiment with balloons and carriers of different sizes and shapes. What model works best? Choose your best contraption; then, set up two string routes so you and a friend can race your fastest rockets.

Upward Bound

Have a grown-up help you set up a floor-to-ceiling (or rock-to-tree-limb) route. Will your rocket travel to the ceiling?

5... 4...
3... 2...
1...

Push Away

Inflate and tie the neck of one balloon and place it in a plastic-bag carrier at the back end of your rocket launcher. Now, blast your rocket with a second balloon. As your rocket shoots forward, watch what happens to the tied balloon.

More Power to You!

Use kitchen-made carbon dioxide gas to actually power a boat!
Make one from a plastic soda bottle with a tight-fitting cap.

1. Ask a grown-up to poke a small hole near the bottom edge of the bottle. Insert a straw, leaving about 1 inch (2.5 cm) hanging out. Use modeling clay to seal the area around the straw.

2. Pour about a tablespoon (15 ml) of baking-soda onto a 4-inch (10-cm) square of tissue paper or paper towel. Roll it up and twist the ends so it looks like a party favor. (Be sure this baking soda packet is narrow enough to slide into the bottle's mouth).

3. Pour about ¼ cup (50 ml) vinegar into the top of the bottle, tilting the bottle so the vinegar doesn't leak out the straw.

4. Ready for the launch? Slip the packet into the bottle. Quickly twist on the bottle cap. Set the boat in a tub of water and watch it go.

Nice work! You've just fueled your boat with carbon dioxide gas. As the gas shoots out and against the water, the boat speeds forward. Action, reaction!

Off to Space!

What do balloons, jets, and rockets have in common? Newton's third law of motion, of course! Rocket fuel burns so hot that gases inside the rocket's combustion chamber rapidly expand. They rush out through an exhaust nozzle just like air shooting out of the neck of a balloon, producing enough force to propel a jet or send a rocket straight up. The amazing action is the escaping gases. And what an incredible reaction — a blastoff in the opposite direction, strong enough to force a rocket into outer space!

DISCOURAGED? NO WAY!

When he was only 5 years old, Robert Goddard rubbed zinc from a battery onto the soles of his shoes, thinking he could create sparks powerful enough to send him skyward. It didn't work, but that didn't bother him one bit. He kept on experimenting. Once, he tried to get a hydrogen-filled aluminum balloon afloat. Another idea he had was to launch a bow-and-arrow-like contraption. Although none of these gizmos worked, Goddard refused to get discouraged. He read books about space travel and filled many notebooks and journals with his wonderful ideas!

Childhood experiments paved the way for Goddard's eventual success. In 1926 he launched the first liquid-fuel-propelled rocket, contributing to space-flight science with a big bang!

Whose Bright Idea?

ROBERT GODDARD

Team Up!

Although you may think inventors work alone, no one really does. Most new inventions grow from past inventions. Inventing often takes the work of many minds. Sometimes people team up together and sometimes they "team up" over time.

We can thank a lot of people for getting us flying through the air. The Wright brothers (see page 17) studied the winged gizmos of others to invent a plane that could be steered and motorized. Others thought of ways to make airplanes and jets stronger, lighter, and faster. And what about *space* flight? Robert Goddard got us using liquid fuel. But landing on the moon is so complicated that whole teams of people worked together, each adding their special area of knowledge.

Join the storm — the brainstorm, that is. Do you have a problem to solve or a better way of doing something to share? Gather a few friends and brainstorm together, tossing ideas out like watermelon seeds. Get your ideas flowing and then jot them all down. There's no right or wrong. Each person's ideas count!

Paddle Power!

Propel this paddle boat propel forward, according to Newton's third law of motion.

Let's build it!

1. Lay the carton on its side. Cut a rectangle about 2¼ inches x 3 inches (5.5 cm x 7.5 cm) from the top. This becomes your boat's paddle.

2. Poke two holes in the opposite side-facing panels, one on each side, each 1 inch (2.5 cm) from the bottom and 1 inch (2.5 cm) in from the edge.

Tools & Supplies

◎ Clean 1-quart (1-L) milk carton
◎ Scissors
◎ 2 pencils or chopsticks
◎ Rubber band
◎ Tape

3. Poke a pencil or chopstick about 2 inches (5 cm) into each side hole and loop a rubber band around the two ends that stick out. The rubber band will hold the pencils together while pressing their other ends up against the inside walls of the carton.

🌸 *Gizmos & Gadgets* 🌸

4. Place the cardboard paddle in the rubber band. Cut the cardboard to fit so that it can turn freely between the pencils. Tape it in place.

5. Wind the paddle away from the milk carton. Hold the paddle in the twisted band. Place the boat in water and release the paddle. What happens? Look at the direction the paddle is turning and the direction the boat is moving.

Cool, huh?

Ship Ahoy!

How'd That Happen?

Can you name the action and reaction? The paddle pushes against the water as it turns, making the boat move in an opposite direction, following Newton's third law of motion.

Science Clues

Where's the power? Learn how a rubber band stores energy on page 114.

!? Step out of a boat: The boat backs away from the pier! Can you use Newton's third law to help you figure out why?

A "Fair" Idea

GEORGE WASHINGTON GALE FERRIS, JR.

Fast Physics

Pool Table Physics

First baseball and now pool. Newton could have been quite a ball player!

Try this: Roll one orange into another. Sure, the one that's hit moves, but what happens to the roller? It stops or even rolls backward. The roller receives an opposite force from the orange it hits, making the roller change direction or stop. Action (the hit), reaction (stop or move back). Think of Newton's third law the next time you play pool!

action

impact

reaction

Inventive minds often see something new in something old. George Washington Gale Ferris, Jr. grew up in Nevada near the Carson River. As a boy he enjoyed watching the paddle boats floating by. Later, when he was a grown-up, he remembered what he'd seen. "I'll bet there's another way a turning wheel can give folks a ride!" he thought. Does his name give you a clue about what he invented? George Washington Gale Ferris, Jr. Hmm. Not the George wheel, but ... !

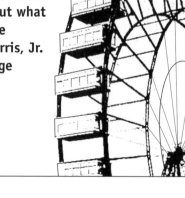

It's a Motion Commotion!

Okay, Newton fans. Here are the three rules of motion happening right before your eyes. Now you and your friends come up with your own examples.

1. Without a force (push or pull), an object either stays still or continues moving in a straight line at the same speed.

3. For every action, there is an equal and opposite reaction.

2. A force on an object sets it in motion or changes how it moves. The greater the force, the greater the change.

Get a Grip!

Kick a ball, roll down a grassy slope, or coast on your bike. Why don't you, the ball, and the bike just keep moving forever? After all, we just got moving with Newton — "an object in motion remains in motion …"

It's the gripping force of **friction** in action! When things rub together, like the ball or you on some grass, friction works to bring them to a stop. So whether you're swimming through water, parachuting from a plane, or simply walking along, friction is there to slow you down. What a rub!

The gizmos in this chapter work by adding friction … or by taking it away. Explore this amazing force by making contraptions that stop and go according to their "friction condition"!

Jitter-Critter

What stops the drop of this jittering spider? Make this critter contraption to see!

Tools & Supplies
◎ Pushpin
◎ Cork
◎ Thumbtacks
◎ Pipe cleaner
◎ Large paper clip
◎ Broom or mop with a long, even handle

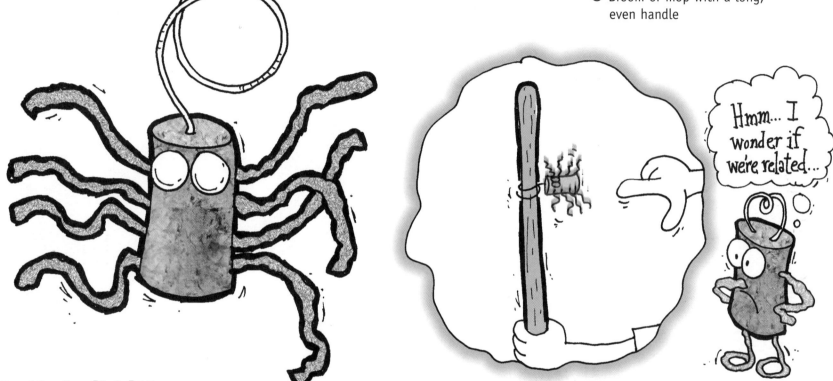

Hmm... I wonder if we're related...

Let's build it!

1. Use a pushpin to make four holes in each side of a cork. Insert half lengths of pipe cleaner into each hole and bend them to look like legs. Add thumbtack eyes.

2. Straighten a large paper clip. Wind it around the end of a broom handle about $1^1/2$ times to make a coil, leaving about 1 inch (2.5 cm) of the wire extending out. Poke this "arm" into the end of the spider's body.

3. Carefully slip the spider gizmo onto the broom handle. Hold the broom upright with one hand and gently press down on the spider. Watch your jitter-critter jiggle its way down the pole!

Tip: You may need to loosen or tighten the coil to get just the right action.

How'd That Happen?

Stop the Drop

The forces of *friction* and *gravity* (see page 49) create the jitter-critter's stop-and-drop motion. When you slide the gizmo to the top of the handle, you'd expect it to drop down, thanks to gravity, right? Instead, the weight of the cork tilts the coil so its edge rubs against the dowel. There's enough friction (rubbing) to keep the gizmo from falling.

Meanwhile, the springy wire arm sets the gizmo moving slightly back and forth. Sometimes the coil lines up so that the gizmo falls straight down (hello, gravity!); at other times the coil tilts and catches on the handle (fantastic friction again), so that the gizmo stops for an instant, and then goes on!

Fast Physics

More or Less?

Put a sneaker on one foot and a sock on the other. Slide each foot across a bare floor. Compare the action. Sometimes, more friction is better. The rough tread on the bottom of your sneaker is designed to increase friction, keeping you from slipping as you run.

Other times, less friction is best. Touch the bottom of a snow ski. Can you feel the smooth surface designed to limit friction for a longer glide?

Rough materials produce more friction than smooth. But even the smoothest objects (like a marble on a polished floor) have microscopic "bumps" that rub against each other and slow movement to a stop, eventually.

MINI-JIGGLER

Use friction and gravity to stop and drop any critter down a pole!

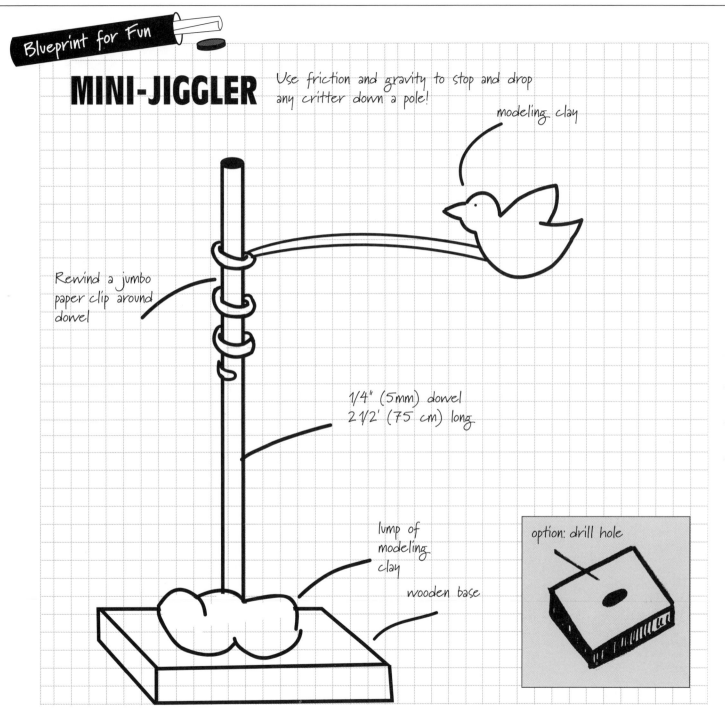

modeling clay

Rewind a jumbo paper clip around dowel

1/4" (5mm) dowel
2 1/2' (75 cm) long

lump of modeling clay

wooden base

option: drill hole

Science Speak!

Friction is a force that slows the motion when one solid object rubs against another, or when a solid object moves through liquids (like a boat moving through water) or gases (like a parachute moving through air).

A GRIPPING INVENTION

Those burrs that sometimes cling to your socks after an outdoor walk are real grippers. Most folks would be annoyed by all that friction. Not George de Mestral.

About 50 years ago, picking burrs from his socks only made him curious. How do these things stick so securely? Careful observation under a microscope gave him the answer: tiny hooks! Could he somehow apply a principle of nature ("sticker hooks") to a different situation — such as keeping his clothes together? Persistence paid off! After many years of work, he invented a totally new product that keeps clothing fastened tight: Velcro! The word is French for *velours* (velvet) and *crochet* (hook).

Think of de Mestral's inventive mind the next time you close your coat sleeve with Velcro!

!?

If a cat's kiss feels like sandpaper, then a panther's kiss could tear your skin! What causes feline tongues to make so much friction? They're covered with a field of tiny spikes. They sure come in handy for brushing fur, slurping water, and cleaning off bones. But, beware. The larger the cat, the rougher the tongue. *Meow!*

They've Got Sole!

You can learn a lot about friction by exploring the soles of footgear. Check these out and think about their uses: basketball shoes, hiking boots, cleated shoes for baseball and soccer, ballet slippers, rain boots, skates, snowshoes, crampons.

Which would *you* choose to climb Mount Everest?

Stop-and-Gobot

Watch the force of friction at work as you control this slip-and-grip robot!

Tools & Supplies
◎ Small cardboard boxes
◎ Recycled paper and other items
◎ Aluminum foil
◎ 2 index cards
◎ Tape
◎ String

Let's build it!

1. Create a robot body from a small cardboard box. Use your imagination to give the robot legs, a head, and antennae from other recycled items. Wrap the body sections in foil to give the gobot a metallic look if you wish.

2. Fold an index card as shown. Center it on a second index card and tape it in place. Now, fold about $1/2$ inch (1 cm) down on the ends of the second card. Punch a hole at the center and near the fold at each end. Tape the card to the back of the robot body.

3. Thread about a yard (1 m) of string through the holes and over the ridge created by the first index card.

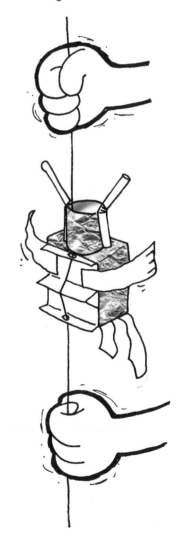

4. Stretch the string tightly with both hands, holding it perpendicular to the floor. Position the gobot at the top. Does it move?

5. Relax the string slightly. Now what happens? By tightening and loosening the string, you can control the gobot's movement downward.

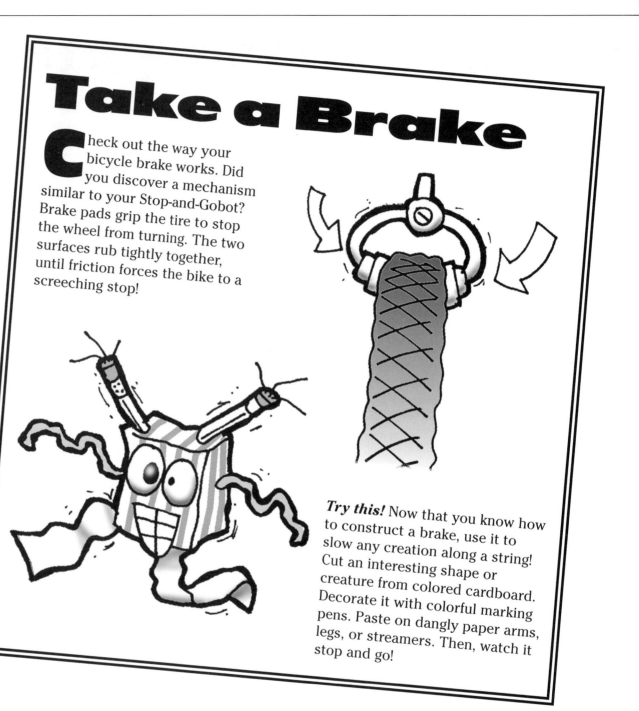

STOP RIGHT THERE!

Tightening the string forces it to rub against the cardboard ridge. And when the string grips the ridge, it stops the gobot from moving. When the string is relaxed, it barely touches the ridge, so the gobot slips freely. That's friction for you: The tighter the rub, the greater the grip, and the better the stopping power!

Take a Brake

Check out the way your bicycle brake works. Did you discover a mechanism similar to your Stop-and-Gobot? Brake pads grip the tire to stop the wheel from turning. The two surfaces rub tightly together, until friction forces the bike to a screeching stop!

Try this! Now that you know how to construct a brake, use it to slow any creation along a string! Cut an interesting shape or creature from colored cardboard. Decorate it with colorful marking pens. Paste on dangly paper arms, legs, or streamers. Then, watch it stop and go!

A World Without Friction?

To get an idea of how impossible life would be in a world without friction, try opening a jar of jelly with soapy hands! No way, right? Just imagine ...

For starters, no one could walk. It's the friction between the bottoms of our feet and the ground that keeps us from slipping as we take each step. And the friction between tires and the road keeps cars on course. Unless slipping, sliding, crashing, and colliding are your thing, a friction-free world is no place to be!

Be a friction detective. Walk around your home or school with an observant eye (and hand) to discover where designers have added friction to their inventions — and where they've tried to eliminate it! Here are some clues:

- Look for treads, ridges, and other "grippy" materials.
- Check out handles, the bottoms of furniture legs, boots, and rugs.
- Look carefully at different kinds of sports equipment.

Friction-Fighting Pants

Way out West in the 1850s, friction's wear was raising havoc with miners. Their pants were wearing out too quickly! When Levi Strauss tried using canvas to make a sturdier pair of pants, he had no idea they'd still be in style more than a hundred years later. He was simply trying to solve a problem with what he had on hand: the canvas to make tents and wagon covers for gold prospectors.

Word spread rapidly about Levi's remarkably sturdy pants, and he soon found himself in the clothing manufacturing business! Levi switched from canvas to denim and riveted the pockets to make them strong enough to hold all those heavy gold nuggets. (He must have known something about gravity, too.) Although most folks don't mine for gold today, we still buy plenty of Levi jeans!

Whose Bright Idea?

LEVI STRAUSS

!? Even a violinist uses friction. Rubbing the bow with rosin causes it to grip the strings as it moves, producing a sweet sound! And, friction is a music maker for crickets, too. Rubbing their wings together makes a chirping summer serenade.

Lazy Susan

Discover how less friction can be more — more treats, that is! This handy contraption spins a snack!

Tools & Supplies
◎ Marbles, all the same size
◎ 2 jar lids without inside ridges, one slightly larger than the other
◎ Modeling clay
◎ Plastic plate
◎ Snacks

Let's build it!

1. Place just enough marbles inside the smaller lid to fill it.

2. Use a lump of modeling clay to attach the upside-down top of a larger lid to the bottom of a plastic plate. Be sure the plate is centered (in the middle). Or, if the plate is a castoff, have a grown-up hot-glue it in place.

3. Set the larger lid onto the marble-filled smaller lid.

4. Fill the plate with snacks. Set your lazy Susan in the center of the table and let friends reach for each snack by spinning the plate. Yum!

Slick Trick

How'd That Happen?

Marbles keep the two lids from touching, so the top lid can spin freely. Like bearings in a machine, they reduce friction for a smoother action.

VERY CLEVER!

The problem. The pyramid builders back in ancient Egypt were faced with a hefty friction situation: How could they move stones to the top of a pyramid? (Remember, there were no cranes back then!)

The solution. The clever Egyptians built earth ramps around the pyramid and hauled the stones on log *sledges* — a sled on logs. What seemed impossible became doable once friction was reduced!

Make your own sledge. Test out the Egyptians' technique.
First, try pushing a book across a smooth floor or tabletop using your pinkie. Now, place six round pencils equally spaced beneath the book and push again. Feel the difference? What else could you move with your pencil sledge? Compare the action of the pencil sledge to the lazy Susan.

The Friction Foilers

Little balls or rollers, called **bearings**, in machines work like the marbles between the lids of the lazy Susan and the pencils of your sledge. And guess what else? You rely on bearings for the swift action of your skates! (In fact, roller skates used to be called "ball bearing skates.") These bearings move in a track between outer and inner steel rings, allowing parts to move with less friction.

But even with bearings, rubbing and heat from friction can wear machine parts out — or even cause them to melt! **Lubricants** to the rescue! These slippery substances (like oil and grease) fill the spaces between bumps that make surfaces rough. Instead of parts rubbing against parts, they rub against the smoother lubricant! Pretty slick, huh?

Science Speak!

A *lubricant* is the slippery stuff (like the oil you put on your bike chain) that lets surfaces slide over each other with less friction. This friction fighter makes movement between moving parts easier.

Fast Physics

RUB-A-DUB

Rub your dry hands together. What do you feel? Friction transforms the energy of your moving hands into heat! Press your hands more closely together as you rub. Is more heat produced?

Now, coat your hands with soap and rub them together again. Which way feels slippery? Which way feels grippy and warm? Soap works as a *lubricant!* Now you know why a tight ring will slip right off your finger if you add soap.

SPLURT!

SPLORT!

SIZZLIN' HOT!

What force can transform motion into heat — making the cockpit of a race car get so hot that drivers must wear protective cooling vests? Friction ... it's hot stuff!

SLOSH SLOSH

SPLISH SPLASH

Thinking About Ink

Whose Bright Idea?

LÁSZLÓ BIRO

Fast Physics

Roll'em!

Set a lid on top of a handful of marbles. Push this contraption across the floor. Unlike a toy car that goes only forward or back, this crazy gizmo rolls in any direction! Compare this movement to the way a lid moves when pushed without marbles beneath. Can you feel the friction difference?

As a magazine reporter, László Biro did lots of writing. "There must be a better writing contraption than this," he thought as he stopped to refill his fountain pen and deal with ink leaks and spills.

The fast-drying ink used in the printing presses gave him an idea. Why not put this ink inside a pen? Great idea, but the new kind of ink didn't flow through the old kind of fountain pen. He had to refine the pen's design. By placing a ball at the tip instead of a point, the ink could be spread out — just as a paint roller spreads paint.

Pick up one of the billions of ballpoint pens around today to see how well a ball helps *your* words flow!

IT'S COLD OUT THERE!

Whose Bright Idea?

CHESTER GREENWOOD

!? What slippery, sticky goo helps a slug get around? Mucus! It's slippery to reduce friction between the slug and rough surfaces. It's sticky to increase friction so the slug can creep against surfaces. Double-action mucus — it's super stuff!

Rubbing his ears to keep them warm while ice skating just wasn't an option for young Chester Greenwood. He just had to think of a way to keep his ears warm so he could stay out late and skate!

In 1873, at the age of 15, Chester became a problem solver and an inventor. He bent a looped frame from baling wire. His grandmother joined in the inventing adventure by sewing beaver fur on the outside of each loop and velvet on the side that would touch his ears. Chester placed the contraption on his ears and headed outside in the freezing air to test it out. Not only did it work for him, but others were eager to buy the snug "earflaps." Time passed, he improved the design, and by 1936 he had a factory producing 400,000 earmuffs each year!

Be a Problem Solver!

Ever hear the old-time saying "Necessity is the mother of invention"? It's still true today. Problems (such as how to keep your ears warm) give birth to creative solutions (Chester Greenwood's earflaps).

Can you think of a problem you sometimes have that's waiting to be solved? Maybe how to keep your mittens from getting separated and lost? Or, how to keep track of your swimming goggles?

Blow-and-Go Parachute

Use friction to give this little sky diver a gentle landing back to Earth!

Let's build it!

The sky diver

1. Roll a quarter sheet of paper into a tight cone 4 inches (10 cm) long and 1½ inches (3.5 cm) across at its opening. Tape the cone together. Snip the bottom edge even.

2. Decorate with markers to look like a sky diver.

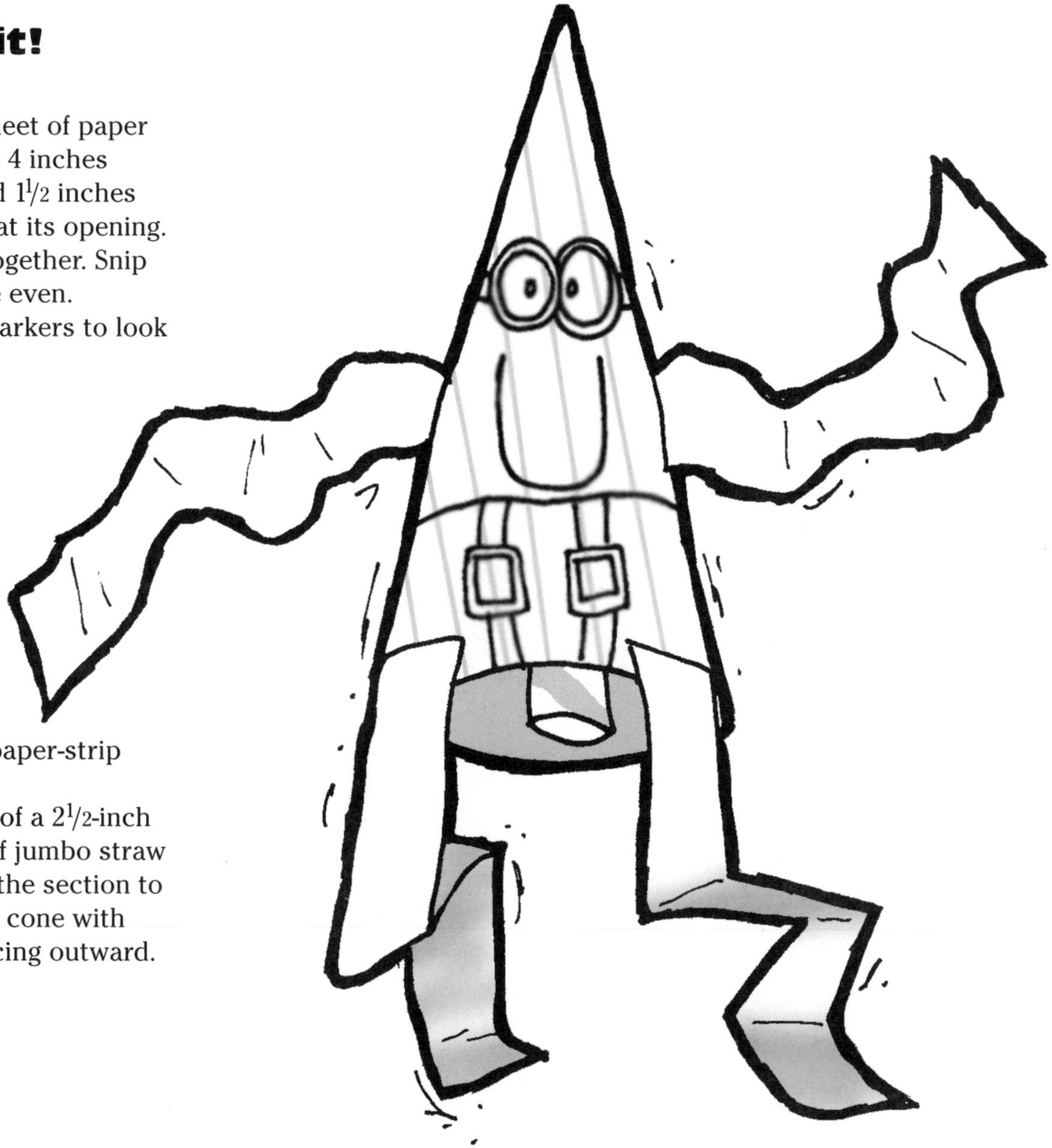

3. Tape on folded-paper-strip arms and legs.

4. Seal off one end of a 2½-inch (6-cm) section of jumbo straw with tape. Tape the section to the inside of the cone with the open end facing outward.

Tools & Supplies

◎ Paper
◎ Tape
◎ Scissors
◎ Colored markers
◎ Paper strips
◎ Jumbo and regular-sized plastic drinking straws
◎ Plastic grocery bag
◎ Thread

The parachute

1. Cut an 8-inch (20-cm) square from the plastic bag to make the canopy.

2. Cut four 8-inch (20-cm) lengths of thread and tie or tape one to each corner of the square.

3. Tie the other ends of the threads together and tape onto the top of the cone.

The launch

Insert the narrow straw into the straw section already taped inside the cone. Set the point of the cone at the center of the canopy, so that the canopy drapes gently around the cone. Point the straw to the sky and blow sharply through it.

Air's There

How'd That Happen?

What force slows a parachute? Friction between the air and the falling chute traps air beneath the chute. Although the downward force of Earth's gravity (see page 49) eventually pulls the sky diver to the ground, the upward resisting force of trapped air against the chute ensures a more gentle descent.

!? Imagine a parachute popping out of the back of a race car as it's stopping. Yup, it's for real! Sometimes brakes just aren't good enough.

In Search of the Perfect Parachute

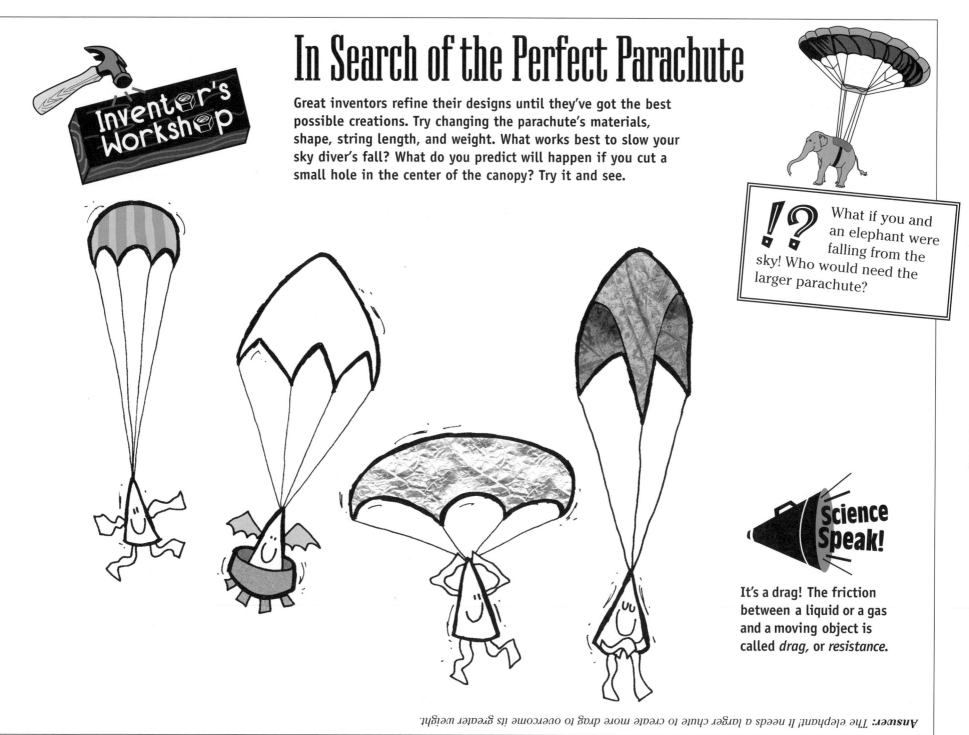

Great inventors refine their designs until they've got the best possible creations. Try changing the parachute's materials, shape, string length, and weight. What works best to slow your sky diver's fall? What do you predict will happen if you cut a small hole in the center of the canopy? Try it and see.

Inventor's Workshop

!? What if you and an elephant were falling from the sky! Who would need the larger parachute?

Science Speak!

It's a drag! The friction between a liquid or a gas and a moving object is called *drag,* or *resistance.*

Answer: *The elephant! It needs a larger chute to create more drag to overcome its greater weight.*

Streamlining is shaping an object for least resistance as it travels through water or air.

!? ◎ The sailfish zips through ocean waters at a cool 60 mph (96 kph). That's the speed limit on most freeways! This fish knows about streamlining: It folds its fins into grooves on its body when it wants to reach high speeds.

◎ Imagine you are competing in the world-famous Tour de France bicycle race on a new high-speed bike. How should you ride to reduce drag, upright or crouched over?

Answer: *Crouched over to reduce the drag.*

Streamlined Design

While sky divers depend on friction, other travelers would rather avoid it. Friction can slow down an aircraft. Clever aerospace engineers design the shape of aircraft to slip through the air producing as little friction as possible. They look to nature for inspiration: The sleek bodies of fish or birds are shapes that reduce resistance. What others can you think of?

FAR FROM FRICTION?

Even with the most streamlined design, high-tech ball bearings, and slickest lubricants, there's always some friction remaining. So a machine will eventually stop, unless it gets more fuel (energy) to keep it going. On Earth, that is.

Out in space, where there is no air to create friction, things are different. Once free from Earth's gravity and atmosphere, a spacecraft can move without ever filling up for fuel again! Scientists use this freedom from friction to send space probes on voyages to planets far away.

It's a bird, it's a plane, it's a ... Hovercraft!

Watch this gizmo zoom across the floor on a cushion of air!

Tools & Supplies
◎ Scissors
◎ Plastic soda bottle
◎ Disposable plastic bowl
◎ Marker or pencil
◎ Tape

Let's build it!

1. With a grown-up's help, cut the neck from the plastic soda bottle, leaving about a 1-inch (2.5-cm) skirt.

2. Stand the neck in the center of a plastic bowl and trace around the spout edge with the pencil or marker.

3. With a grown-up's help, cut out a circle slightly larger than your tracing.

Push the neck through the hole so it pokes out from the bottom side of the bowl. (You may need to readjust the hole size.) Seal with tape if the neck doesn't fit snugly.

4. Set your hovercraft on a smooth surface. Now, blow through the bottle neck and watch the action!

Cushy Air

How'd That Happen?

Would you rather run a race through water or through air? (Imagine swimming across a pool while someone else is running beside it.) Even for the best swimmers, swimming is slower because there's more drag (see page 43) when moving through water than through air.

Clever inventors used this same observation to design contraptions that travel across water while avoiding its drag. On a real hovercraft, fans drive air beneath the craft, creating an air cushion.

Moving on a cushion of air produces less friction than moving through water, so a hovercraft can travel with more speed than if it sat in the water.

Your hovercraft travels across a tabletop in a similar way: on a cushion of air!

!? Ever wonder why Olympic swimmers crop their hair, wear tight caps, and shave their bodies? Sleek is best when you want to fight water resistance. Just look at a dolphin's skin. It's super-smooth for speedy swimming.

Inventor's Workshop

Hover-Mania!

Lighten Up

Do you see every discarded container as a potential hovercraft? Build a lightweight body from deli tubs, cups, food trays, and lids of all shapes and sizes.

So Simple

- *Bottle neck.* Cut a plastic soda bottle about 1 inch (2.5 cm) below the neck. Be sure the edge is cut straight so that it stands evenly on the floor.
- *Paper cone.* Roll a sheet of paper into a cone shape. Seal the edge with tape. Cut the bottom edge even. Snip the top to create a hole to blow into.
- *Funnel.* Turn a funnel upside down and blow through the narrow part.

Get Air

- Channel air through a cardboard paper tube, a rolled-up piece of paper, or simply a hole within the body.
- Use a blow dryer on the cool setting to blow air down the neck.
- Tape a 2-inch (5-cm) paper skirt onto the bottom edge of the body to collect even more air.

Which design makes the best hovercraft? Can it also work across a tub of still water?

RALPH SAMUELSON

Water Ski Success

Be Persistent!

Inventors don't give up. Creating inventions is a process of trial and error. Usually things don't work out just right the first few times. With all the testing and redesigning inventing requires, it's easy to give up. A clever mind, like Ralph Samuelson's, uses each failure to get closer to success.

The thousands of folks who love to zoom across lakes on water skis each summer have a persistent teenager to thank. In 1922, Ralph Samuelson had a clever idea. Why not try to ski on water instead of snow? He put on his snow skis and held onto a rope attached to a boat. But as the boat pulled forward, his narrow skis could not support his weight, and the feat only produced laughs from the crowds watching on shore.

Next, Ralph tried slats from a wood barrel. Again no luck, but he didn't give up. From each failure, he learned something about how to improve the design. Shaping pine boards himself, he created the first successful water skis. Other improvements such as a better towrope, a faster speedboat, and improved skis helped make this smooth sport so popular today!

All Fall Down!

Shoot a basketball, pour some juice, or dive into a pool. What happens? The force of **gravity** pulls everything down. It's the same glorious force that holds oceans on Earth and keeps us from falling off. Thank goodness for Earth's gravitational pull!

You can put gravity to use (as in pendulum clocks and slides) or defy it (think of airplanes and elevators). But one thing's for certain: You just can't ignore a force so powerful. Play with this downward pull by using gravity to power a boat, bring a dino to life, and tumble a troll head over heels!

Up-and-Down Dino

Use the force of gravity to raise and lower the neck of this mighty creature contraption!

Let's build it!

1. Trace the dino shape onto the cereal box cardboard and cut it out. Cut the base from corrugated cardboard. Add dino details and grass with markers.

2. Punch holes in the head and body where shown. Make the weight with string and a metal nut.

Tools & Supplies
◎ Pencil
◎ Cereal box cardboard
◎ Scissors
◎ Corrugated cardboard
◎ Colored markers
◎ Hole punch
◎ String
◎ Metal nut
◎ 4 plastic beads and thread
◎ Needle
◎ Glue

handle

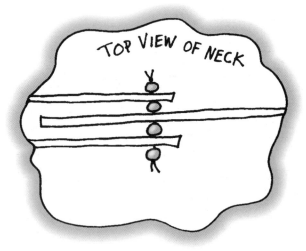

TOP VIEW OF NECK

Cut out (use for handle)

3. Assemble the neck using beads and thread.
4. Fold the tabs and glue them onto the base.
5. To operate the gizmo, hold the handle section of the base, and move it so that the nut swings back and forth. Watch your dino in action!

Heavy Head

How'd That Happen?

What's happening as the nut swings beneath the dino's head? The heavy nut adds weight to the front of the gizmo, pulling the dino's head downward. As the nut swings beneath the dino's body, repositioning the weight, the head pops back up.

!?

Why is it easier to jump off a chair than back on?

A HEAVY SUBJECT

Picture a bowling ball and a foam ball, both the same size. Which would be easier to toss? Flinging the foam is no problem, but the bowling ball is difficult to lift! Why? The bowling ball has more *mass* — more "stuff" or *matter* in it for gravity to pull on. That pull of gravity gives things *weight*. If it's too heavy to lift off the ground, gravity wins over your muscle power!

Science Speak!

◎ *Matter* is anything that takes up space and has weight.
◎ *Mass* is the amount of matter something has.
◎ *Weight* is the pull of gravity on the mass. More mass means more weight, because there's more for gravity to pull on!

Answer: *Gravity pulls you down when you jump off the chair, but you're fighting gravity when you jump back up.*

Gravity Play!

Ever wonder how kids powered their toys before the days of batteries, electric power, and computer chips? They relied on natural forces — like gravity! The Up-and-Down Dino is modeled after a more complicated wooden gizmo made hundreds of years ago by European toy makers. It was probably brought to America by children unwilling to leave their favorite toy behind. Like the dino, a flock of pecking hens took turns raising and lowering their heads as a heavy wooden ball swung beneath them. Then — and now — it's gravity in action!

Can you see how gravity is at work in these other toy classics?

Critter Catch

Use markers to decorate a paper-towel tube to look like a critter with an open mouth. Paste on colored paper details if you like. Punch a hole near the edge of the mouth. Crumple a piece of aluminum foil into a ball that easily fits into the critter's mouth. Attach about 2 feet (60 cm) of string to the ball and tie the other end to the hole.

To play: Hold the bottom of the tube. Push up on the tube to hurl the ball into the air. Now, let gravity help you to catch it in the critter's mouth.

Ring Thing

Cut a head shape from corrugated cardboard and cut out a 2-inch-wide (5-cm) circle mouth. Decorate the head to look like a monster. Tie a yard (1 m) of cord to the monster's mouth. Thread four canning jar bands onto the string, and then tie the free end to the bottom of a foot-long (30-cm) stick.

To play: Hold the bottom of the stick. Stack the rings and the monster face onto the stick. Hurl them into the air; then with the help of gravity, catch them back on the stick, with the monster mouth last.

Toying With Gravity

Mistakes upset some folks, but for alert people, they can be an inspiration. Take the case of Richard James. One day in 1943, when he was an engineer aboard a U.S. Navy ship, a spring became loose and fell to the floor. Its weird bouncing motion got James wondering, "Would kids enjoy playing with such a toy?" Back home, he perfected the coil and manufactured it as a toy. Can you guess the name of this popular gravity-powered flip-flopper?

Whose Bright Idea?

RICHARD JAMES

A Silly Success

Whose Bright Idea?

Silly Putty

PETER HODGSON

Try as he might, chemist James Wright was never able to create rubber from silicon oil as he had hoped. When he added boric acid, the strange stuff bounced! Not exactly what he had in mind for making boots and tires.

Along came Peter Hodgson in 1949 with a whole new way of looking at things. To Hodgson, Wright's "failure" was a super toy. He stuck it in a plastic egg, and it's been selling as Silly Putty for half a century!

STAY ALERT!

It's easy to see a failure as a failure. It's a challenge to see a failure as a success. But an alert inventor transforms a mistake into something useful. That's just how many inventions came about!

Answer: It's a Slinky!

GALILEO GALILEI

Galileo's Gravity Lab

It makes sense that heavy objects fall faster than light objects, doesn't it? For thousands of years, that's just what people believed. It took someone with a questioning mind to discover what really happens.

More than 400 years ago, Galileo Galilei thought, "I'm not so sure. I'll try it and see." So, from the top of the Leaning Tower of Pisa in Italy, it is said, he dropped cannonballs of different weights. Look out below ... clunk! Galileo carefully observed the results and proved what folks had always believed was not true at all! His law (scientific rule) of gravity states that all objects fall the same distance in the same time, no matter what they weigh. Galileo was a brilliant experimenter and scientist! Now, don't you wonder what made him question this in the first place?

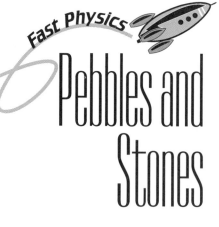

Fast Physics

Pebbles and Stones

Hold a light pebble and a heavier stone over a cookie sheet. Predict which one will hit first when dropped. Listen and watch at cookie-sheet level. Did the weight of the falling object affect its speed? Compare your results with Galileo's.

Fast Physics

Penny Wise

Place two pennies at the edge of a table. At exactly the same moment, flick one outward and let the other fall directly to the floor. Which one hits first?

You just discovered another rule of gravity! *Forward motion has no effect on the downward pull of gravity.* While one penny flies forward and the other drops directly down, gravity pulls both to the floor at the same speed. Are you surprised by this, or does it make sense to you?

Imagine dropping a feather and a hammer from the same height on the moon. Remember, there's no air out there to catch the feather. Would Galileo's experiment still work? You bet! In fact, that's exactly what Apollo 15 astronaut David Scott did in 1971. The whole world watched as the two objects hit the moon's surface at the same time!

Come on, feather!

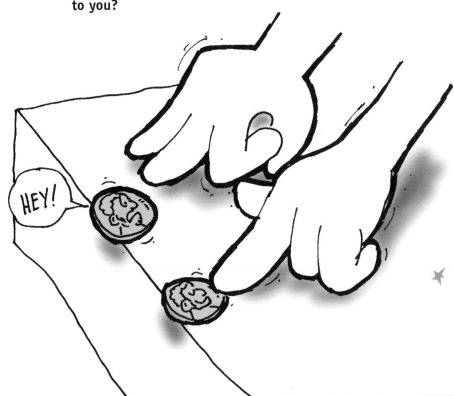

HEY!

Gravity Shuttle

Gravity pulls this space shuttle toward the ground. But not so fast — a spiral of wire forces it to spin along its downward course!

Tools & Supplies

◎ Wire binding (from a discarded spiral-bound notebook)
◎ Broom handle
◎ Scissors
◎ Plastic-ring six-pack holders
◎ Cereal box cardboard
◎ Markers
◎ Tape
◎ Pennies
◎ Stapler
◎ Plastic drinking straw
◎ Paper clip

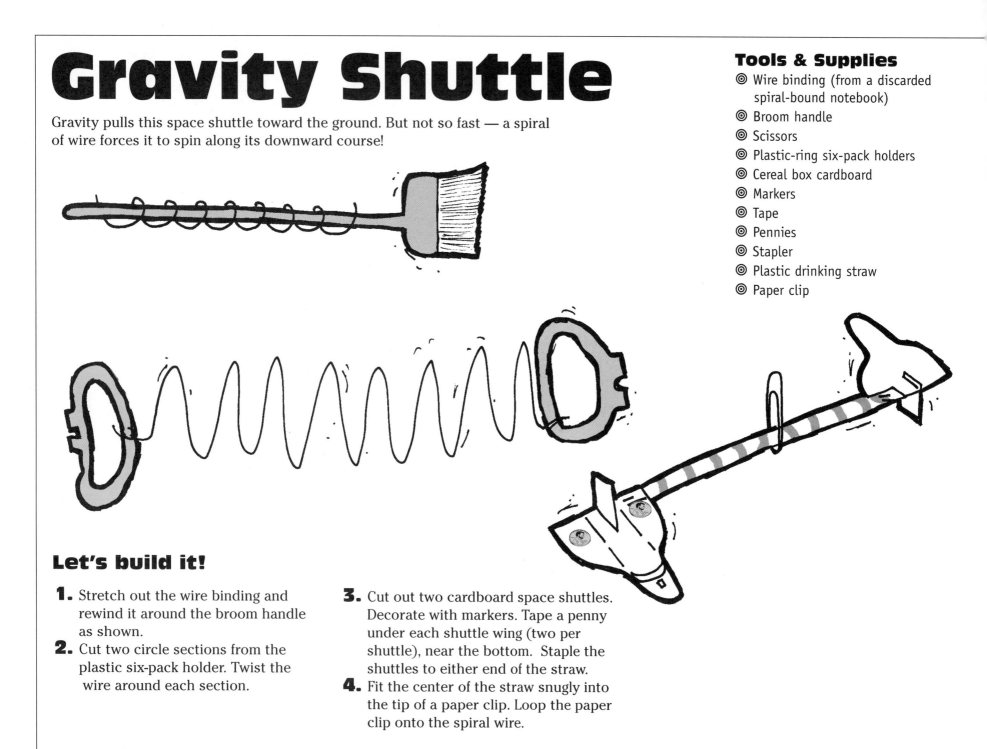

Let's build it!

1. Stretch out the wire binding and rewind it around the broom handle as shown.

2. Cut two circle sections from the plastic six-pack holder. Twist the wire around each section.

3. Cut out two cardboard space shuttles. Decorate with markers. Tape a penny under each shuttle wing (two per shuttle), near the bottom. Staple the shuttles to either end of the straw.

4. Fit the center of the straw snugly into the tip of a paper clip. Loop the paper clip onto the spiral wire.

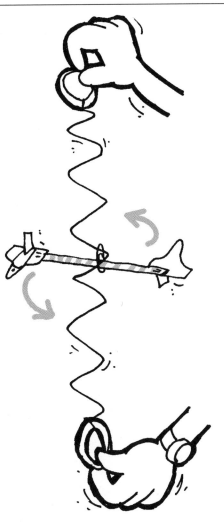

Gravity All Around

Earth's pull is mighty strong, but it isn't the only gravitational force around. Believe it or not, everything has gravity, even you! There's gravitational force between you and your dog, an apple and a banana, your dad and a frying pan.

Surprised? Here's the hitch: You must have lots of mass — like Earth — to make others feel your gravitational pull. Because Earth is so much more massive than anything on it, its pull overwhelms the others. So it's the only gravitational force we actually feel.

5. Place the shuttle at the top end of the spiral. Let go, and watch it zoom and spin towards Earth! (Readjust the twists if necessary.) Now, turn the gizmo upside down and start the gravity action again.

Try this: What else can spiral to the ground? Use your imagination to create a pair of birds (see page 113), airplanes, bats, superheroes (see page 124), or bumblebees to whirl down the gravity spiral. You can get in on the action, too, by spinning *yourself* down a spiral slide at a playground. Enjoy the force!

!? ◎ Do you enjoy exploring tide pools? Thank the moon's gravity. Tides rise and fall twice a day (every 24 hours and 51 minutes) as the moon moves around the earth, tugging on ocean waters.
◎ What's got enough gravitational pull to keep everything in our solar system, from dust and asteroids to moons and planets, orbiting around it? If you said our spectacular star, the sun, you're absolutely right!

May the Force Be With You!

Change your weight by journeying to another planet … or to the moon! Other planets also have gravity, either more or less than here on Earth. You'd weigh even more on Jupiter than you do on Earth! Why? Jupiter has more mass than Earth, so more gravitational pull.

Want to weigh less? Go to the moon. Less mass equals less gravitational pull equals less weight. It's also why astronauts can jump higher on the moon than they can on Earth! Weight depends on how much gravity pulls on your mass, so it changes when the gravitational pull changes.

Here's how much a 60-pound kid would weigh around the solar system:

Earth	60 pounds (27 kg)
Mercury	22 pounds (10 kg)
Venus	53 pounds (24 kg)
Mars	23 pounds (10.5 kg)
Jupiter	140 pounds (64 kg)
Saturn	69 pounds (31 kg)
Uranus	70 pounds (31.5 kg)
Neptune	70 pounds (31.5 kg)
Pluto	8 pounds (3.6 kg)
Earth's moon	10 pounds (4.5 kg)
Sun	16,740 pounds (7,600 kg)

Fast Physics

FREE FALL

Are the falling objects in your house as weightless as astronauts falling through space? Drop this gizmo to see.

Attach a clothespin to either side of a thick rubber band. Hold up one pin. See how gravity pulls the lower pin and band straight? Now drop the gizmo from a high spot (stairwell or balcony). Watch as the gizmo falls: What happens to the band? It goes back to its oval shape. The lower pin (and in fact the entire gizmo) is weightless and can't pull the band straight! You just proved that free fall equals weightlessness!

!? If you wanted to break the galactic high-jump record, would you go to Pluto or Jupiter?

5, 4, 3, 2...

Answer: *Pluto. You'd jump higher because of less gravitational pull.*

Marvelous Marble Ramp

Create an incredible path for a marble; then, set the orb in motion. What pulls the marble from the top of the ramp to the bottom? Good old gravity!

Tools & Supplies

- Large cardboard box
- Empty cereal and cracker boxes
- Paper-towel tubes
- Tape
- Scissors
- Marble
- Bells, cans, and other recyclables

Let's build it!

Here's a chance to really let your inventive imagination run wild! Design a pathway for a marble to follow that wraps around a box base. The ramps can hang on the outside of the box or be suspended inside. Cut corner sections from cereal or cracker boxes and use paper-towel tubes cut in half horizontally for your chutes and ramps. Add your own bells and drops and gaps. Then, tape it all in place and set the ball rolling!

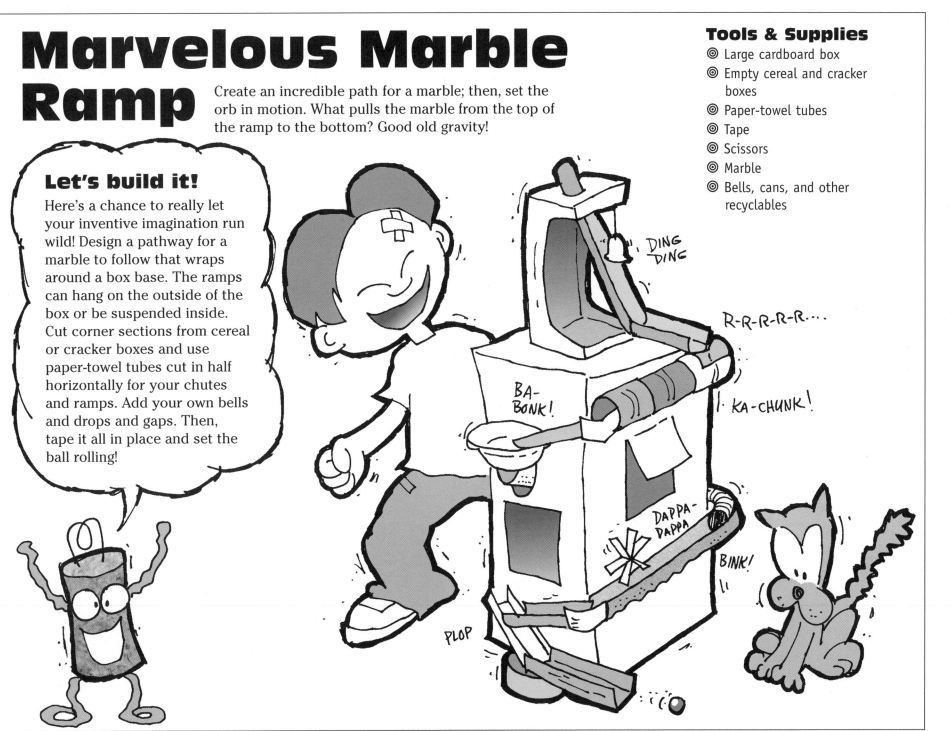

Ramp 'n' Roll

Drop a marble, and all of gravity's force pulls in one direction, directly down. But set a marble on a ramp, and gravity's force is divided. Gravity works to speed the marble down the ramp, while it also works to hold the marble against the ramp's surface. The steeper the ramp, the greater the speeding force, and the weaker the holding force.

In what ways do you zoom down a slope thanks to gravity?

S-t-r-e-t-c-h It

Loop a rubber band around the wheel of a toy car and dangle it directly down. Now set the car on a ramp you make from books and a cookie sheet. Let the car tug at the band. Vary the height of the slope (steep or gentle). Which way stretches the band the most?

GEORGE WASHINGTON CARVER

Peanut Power!

How many uses can you think of for cardboard? We've come up with dozens that have nothing to do with making a box!

Clever people use ordinary materials in extraordinary ways. George Washington Carver was no exception. He thought of more than 300 uses for the peanut — from paint to soap, from shampoo to shaving cream. But the most important use of a peanut to Carver was as a soil builder. Growing up in the South as the son of slaves, he observed how the soil lost all its good nutrients from growing so many cotton crops. His experiments proved that planting peanuts actually enriched the soil. The next time you spread on some peanut butter, think about Carver's creative spirit!

REVAMP THE RAMP

Maxi-Ramp

Construct a fabulous room-sized marble maze. Prop long tubes from wrapping paper and paper towels on chairs, book stacks, or whatever works to make your ramps. Use toilet-paper tubes as connectors. Attach them with masking tape (be sure the larger-diameter tubes face downward). End with a gentle or level ramp. Add marbles and rubber balls, and watch the action!

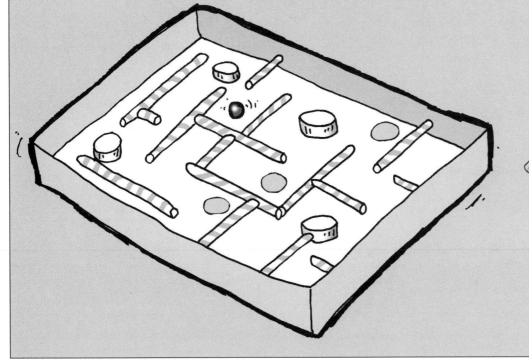

It's A-maze-ing!

Make a miniature marble maze by gluing or taping bent, flexible straws onto a shallow box or lid and adding obstacles like milk jug caps in the path or booby trap holes along the way. Position the marble at the top of slopes you create by continually tilting the maze. Let your sense for how gravity works guide each move.

Mystery Tumbler

Stick a lump of modeling clay to the inside edges of two straight-sided lids. Line up the lumps of clay, and secure the two lids together in that position with masking tape. Place the roller so that the clay lump inside is just past the top of the roller. Let it go, and watch it roll without a push.

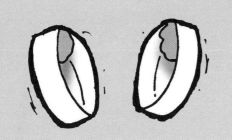

Tiny Tumbler

Trace the pattern on this page onto construction paper. Decorate the outside with markers. Put a marble in the capsule and tape up the seams. Now, prop one end of a dish-towel-covered cookie sheet on a book to create a ramp. Set the tiny tumbler at the top and watch it tumble down.

!? How can a fly creep across the ceiling, defying gravity? A fly has two things going for it: It weighs so little and it has six padded feet covered with hooks — perfect for clinging to those minuscule cracks and crevices up there.

Tumbling Troll

Let gravity help this troll somersault head over heels!

Tools & Supplies
◎ Large cereal box
◎ Scissors
◎ White paper
◎ Colored markers
◎ Hole punch
◎ Pencil, chopstick, or dowel

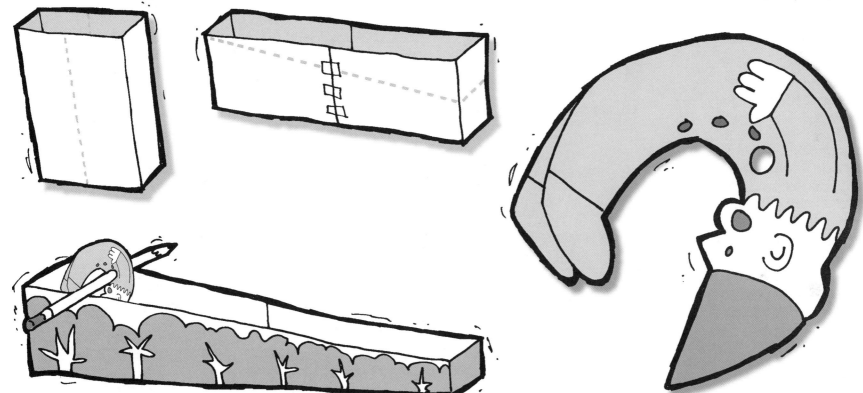

Let's build it!

1. Cut the cereal box in half lengthwise. Attach the two halves together. Create a ramp by cutting a slope from a 4-inch (10-cm) height at one end to 1½ inches (3.5 cm) at the other end.

2. Cover the cardboard with paper. Use markers to decorate with a forest theme. Copy the troll pattern on this page onto cardboard (you can use a section of the cut-off cereal box). Decorate with markers.

3. Punch a hole near the top of your troll's head as shown. Poke the pencil, chopstick, or dowel through the hole.

4. Set the pencil at the top of the ramp. Give it a twist and watch the troll tumble!

Going With Gravity

How'd That Happen?

No matter how mysterious these tumblers look, they can't truly defy gravity. Here's the secret:

◎ The cardboard crescent shape adds weight unevenly to the pencil, causing the fast-slow action of the Tumbling Troll.

◎ The Mystery Tumbler moves forward as the weight of the clay falls downward.

◎ As the marble rolls downward, it pushes against the paper, making the Tiny Tumbler flip-flop along!

Gravity pulls everything downward, including the weight hidden within each of these gizmos!

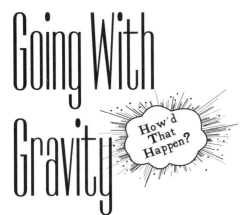

Whose Bright Idea?

JAMES PLIMPTON

On a Roll

It was a pretty strange sight way back in 1760 when Josef Merlin of Belgium rolled into a costume party, playing the violin, with wheeled shoes on his feet. The good news was that he was quite a sensation. (No one had ever seen such a contraption!) The bad news was that a mirror and his violin wound up in smithereens. (Josef couldn't steer or stop!)

Some 100 years later, James Plimpton refined the design, adding cushions between the axles and the foot plates that allowed the skater to steer by shifting his or her weight.

If you've ever had fun roller skating, you know Josef Merlin had the right idea in mind. And what a mind! Like many great inventors, Merlin creatively combined materials (wheels with shoes) in a way never done before to create a totally new product (skates).

THANK YOU, JAMES!

Flow-and-Go Boat

Use gravity's pulling force to power a boat that can go with the flow!

Let's build it!

1. Glue the plates rim to rim.

2. Glue the rim of the bowl to the center of one of the plates.

3. Poke a hole through the side of the cup, near the bottom. Slide a straw through the hole, short elbow first. Seal around the hole with glue.

4. Glue the bottom of the cup to the center of the bowl.

5. Place a book on top of the cup, and let the contraption dry overnight.

6. Set the boat at one end of a tub of water so that the straw is underwater. Fill the cup with water. What happens to the boat?

Anchors Away!

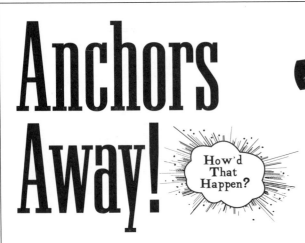

How'd That Happen?

Because of gravity, water always settles to the lowest possible level. This includes the water in the cup of your boat! As the water flows in one direction, it propels the boat in the opposite direction. It's gravity power!

Science Clues

The Flow-and-Go Boat moves according to Newton's third law of motion. Remember? For every action, there's an equal and opposite reaction (see page 19).

Blueprint for Fun

WATER TOWER CLOCK

Stacked soda bottles make a water-action timekeeper!

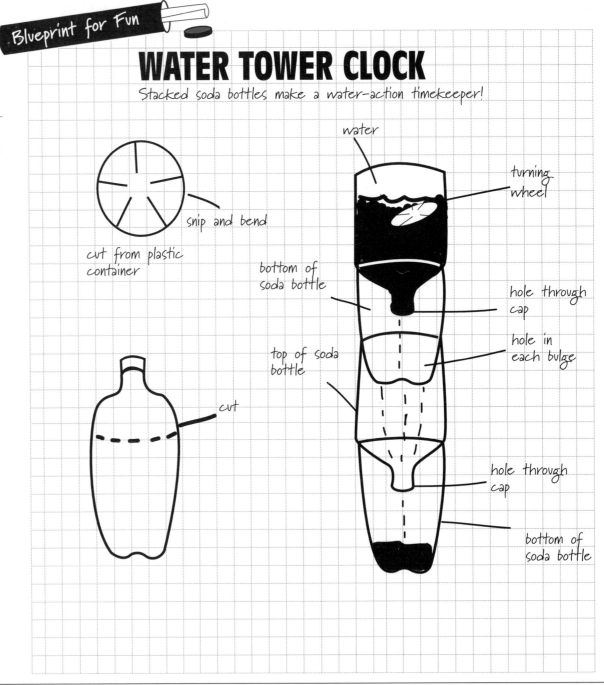

snip and bend

cut from plastic container

cut

water

turning wheel

bottom of soda bottle

hole through cap

top of soda bottle

hole in each bulge

hole through cap

bottom of soda bottle

Gravity's Got Rhythm!

Think about the sound of a dripping faucet. Each drop drips at the same rate, keeping a regular rhythm, thanks to gravity. That's why clocks that used sand or water were some of the world's first timekeepers.

Later on, gravity-powered pendulums were the choice for clock makers. In a pendulum clock, the energy from a swinging pendulum is transferred to a system of gears that move tiny hands to tell the time!

!? Where else do you see water follow gravity's pull? In a waterfall! Imagine water gushing over 3,212 feet (980 m) downward. That's what you see at the world's highest waterfall, Angel Falls in Venezuela!

Science Clues

For more on energy and pendulums, see page 124.

Balancing Act

Have you ever noticed how when you walk on a low, narrow wall or balance beam, you thrust out your arms? You're experiencing the rules of balance in action! While you may not know exactly what balance is, you can tell when you're in balance (wobble-free and upright), and you *definitely* know when you're out of balance! *Ker-plop!*

Discover the basics of balance as you make and design contraptions that wobble, waver, tilt, and finally rest in a perfect harmony of forces. Ah, the beauty of balance!

Slithering Snake

Is it magic or physics? Make this gizmo to find out!

Let's build it!

1. Trace around an old CD on cardboard and cut out the circle. Mark the center point of the circle.

2. Starting from the outer edge (the snake's head), cut out the snake's body by cutting toward the center in a spiral.

3. Use markers to decorate the shape to look like a snake. Add a paper tongue. Glue on tiny bead eyes if you like.

4. Crimp the tail. Set it on a pencil point to balance. What do you predict will happen if you spin the snake? Try it and see!

Tools & Supplies

◎ Pencil
◎ Old CD
◎ Cereal box cardboard
◎ Scissors
◎ Colored markers
◎ Construction paper
◎ Glue
◎ Bead eyes

In the Middle

How'd That Happen?

The balancing point of a disk is at its center. For your slithering snake, that point is at the tip of its tail. It balances because its weight is equally distributed around the point of the pencil. Even spinning the snake won't upset its balance!

Fingertip Fun

What else can you balance? Put your finger under the different numbers of a ruler to find out where the ruler balances best. Now try moving your finger beneath different objects — a Frisbee, ball, book, pair of sunglasses, spoon, and a pencil — until you find the place where each will balance.

What shapes are easiest to balance? Is the object's balancing point where you expected it to be?

Science Speak! Something is *in balance* or *stable* when all forces that push or pull on it cause it to stay still. The *balancing point* is the point at which the object can be supported without falling over.

Fast Physics

Teeter Test

Slowly push a carrot, brush, or other unbreakable object over the edge of a table. Mark the spot just before it starts to teeter. That's its balancing point! Where's the balancing point if you push the object starting from its other end?

P.S. Now do you know why seesaws used to be called teeter-totters?

Magic Trick

Surprise your family members with this trick! Hide a full can of soup in the corner of a shoe box. Set the box on a tabletop so that the empty part hangs far out over the edge and the part with the can is on the table. Put on the shoe box lid. Does the box look like it's about to fall off the table? Only you know why it's in balance!

Tightrope Trials

Notice anything similar about the butterfly and the frog on this page? They are *symmetrical* — what you see on one half of the creature's body is exactly what appears on the other, like you and your reflection when you stand with your shoulder against a mirror. Watch what happens when you put them to the tightrope test!

Make the Balancers

Draw shapes like these on cardboard. Decorate with markers and tape pennies in the spots shown. Set the notch on the tightrope.

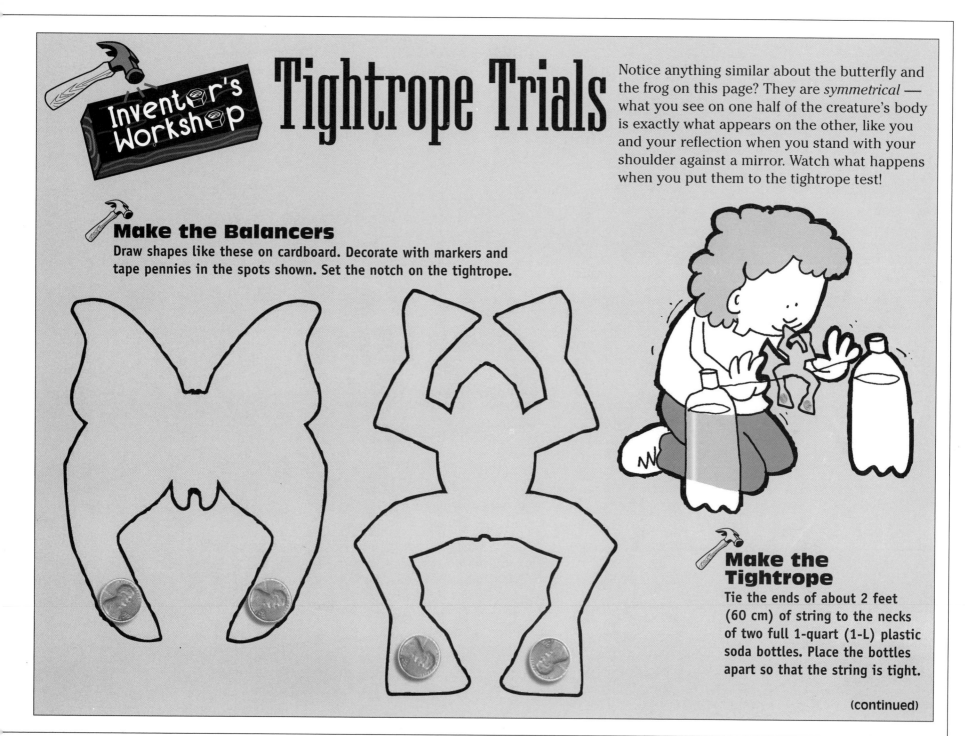

Make the Tightrope

Tie the ends of about 2 feet (60 cm) of string to the necks of two full 1-quart (1-L) plastic soda bottles. Place the bottles apart so that the string is tight.

(continued)

Experiment

- Try balancing the critters with the pennies in different spots. Where must the pennies go in order for the shapes to balance?
- Design your own symmetrical shapes to balance on the tightrope.

It's easy to find the balancing point on a symmetrical object. It's always right along the center!

!? Imagine carrying groceries on your head! It's happening all over the world. Folks in Africa, Asia, and many other lands prefer their heads instead of a backpack or carrying things in their arms. Can you figure out why?

Answer: *The weight of the load is centered, making the carrying easier.*

Perching Parrot

Tools & Supplies

◎ Pencil
◎ Cereal box cardboard
◎ Scissors
◎ Colored markers
◎ Coat hanger
◎ Tape
◎ Large paper clip
◎ Broom or mop with a long, even handle

Let's build it!

1. Draw a parrot shape, like this one, on cardboard, and cut it out.

2. Make a tiny slit and hole near the edge of its belly where shown.

3. Decorate both sides of the shape to look like a parrot. Tape the tails on each side for added weight.

4. Stretch out a coat hanger to form a perch. Slip the parrot onto the perch at the slit, so the wire goes through the hole. Tape the slit closed.

5. Balance the parrot. Add paper clips to the tail or trim the tail as needed to make the parrot sit upright.

6. Try knocking Polly from her perch. What happens?

Perch Point

How'd That Happen?

The weight of the tail makes your parrot balance upright. Give her a push or pull, and you knock her off balance. She swings back and forth until she comes to rest in balance again. **Objects always come to rest at their balancing point.**

IT'S NO PUSH OVER!

Fill one half of a clean eggshell or plastic egg with modeling clay. Push a drinking straw into the clay. For fun, draw a creature on an index card, color it with markers, and cut it out. Punch two holes in the body and thread it onto the straw. Can you push your critter over or make it spin? Watch where it comes to rest.

Feet Feats

Stand with your heels against a wall. Without moving your feet, try to pick up a book on the floor in front of you.

Stand sideways with the side of your foot and shoulder against the wall. Try to lift your other foot.

What's happening? To keep your balance, your body weight needs to be centered over the standing foot, but the wall won't let you "rearrange" your weight (so you fall down). Each time, the wall stops you from rearranging your body weight directly over the standing foot, where it must be in order to keep you in balance.

Now, move away from the wall and perform these same feats. Can you feel how your body weight shifts to keep you in balance?

◎ **Why does a cat have a tail?** Watch a cat climb on furniture and you'll get a clue.

◎ **What do surfboard riders, snowboarders, skiers, skaters, and so many other athletes have in common?**

◎ **Like to bike?** When you're riding a bike, your power, your weight, and your sense of balance keep you from falling over. By keeping those wheels spinning, and adjusting your weight as you move, your bike stays upright, even on the thinnest wheels!

HEY!

Answers: *The cat's tail sways all around, helping it shift its weight to stay in balance. The athletes are all trying to stay upright as they move along tricky surfaces. That's what all that swaying, swerving, and shifting of their body weight is all about.*

Wobble Ball

Catch this ball — if you can!

HAVE A BALL!

Throw the wobble ball into the air and the modeling clay rolls around inside the balloon. The weight of this crazy ball is centered in the very center of that clay ball. **The balloon wobbles as the clay ball moves around, changing the gizmo's center of gravity.**

How'd That Happen?

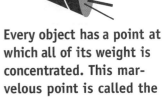

Science Speak!

Every object has a point at which all of its weight is concentrated. This marvelous point is called the *center of gravity.*

Let's build it!

1. Roll a marble-sized piece of modeling clay into a snake shape. Drop it through the neck of a balloon. Roll the balloon back and forth between your palms to reshape the clay back into a ball.

2. Inflate the balloon and tie it at the neck.

3. Throw the wobble ball overhead. Why do you think it moves in such a strange way? Play a game of wobble-ball catch with a friend.

GETTING CENTERED

Often, the center of gravity is right where you'd expect it: in the center of the object! As in an orange. But sometimes the center of gravity can be in the most unusual places. In the wobble ball, it isn't in the center of the ball; it's in the center of the clay. The center of gravity can even be outside the object entirely. In a doughnut, it's right in the center of the hole!

What about you? Stand still, with your feet about a foot apart. Now, stand on one foot. Did your body move at all? As the weight over your foot shifts, your body shifts position in order to stay upright. Whenever you move, your center of gravity changes, too!

Super-Centered Balloon Feet!

You've probably seen these before. Lots of them are made with sand, but in this one, the center of gravity is the cardboard feet. So, make this balloon gizmo with a center of gravity that doesn't move, and compare how it behaves when tossed.

Cut out cardboard feet like the ones shown on this page. Inflate a balloon. Add a face with permanent markers. Slip the neck through the slit between the feet as shown. Toss into the air. With a center of gravity that stays put (the cardboard), you can always count on this fellow to land on his feet!

Get a Lift

Stand between two friends. Have them lift you by your elbows as described below. Which way works best?

1. **Elbows extended forward.**
   Your friends lift at a point *away* from your center of gravity.
2. **Elbows pointed downward and hugged tightly to your sides.**
   Your friends lift you at a point *near* your center of gravity.

Why do you think it's easier for your friends to lift you the second time? Their lifting force works best when it's right under your center of gravity — that special point where all the weight seems concentrated.

The same thing happens to you when you try to lift yourself up out of a chair. Your body shifts so that most of your weight is right over the lifting force — your legs!

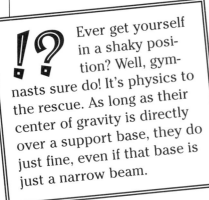

!? Ever get yourself in a shaky position? Well, gymnasts sure do! It's physics to the rescue. As long as their center of gravity is directly over a support base, they do just fine, even if that base is just a narrow beam.

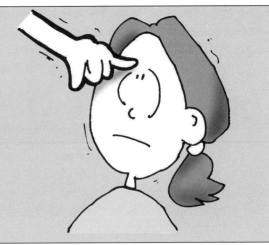

Pinkie Power!
Bet your friend that you can hold her in place with just your pinkie. Have her sit with her back against a chair. Gently put your fingertip on her forehead to keep her from moving forward. Can she lift herself out of the chair?

Amazing Alien

Tools & Supplies
◎ Tape
◎ 4 flexible straws
◎ Cardboard tubes
◎ Index card
◎ Markers
◎ Paper strips
◎ Glue
◎ Toothpick

Can this strange alien truly balance on the point of a toothpick? No way... except the physics way!

Let's build it!

1. Tape straws together above the short elbows.

2. Tape 1-inch-wide (2.5-cm) cardboard tube sections to the long ends of the two center straws. Shorten the two outside straws to form arms.

3. Cut the index card in half lengthwise. Tape the ends together. This will be the alien's head. Use markers to draw the face. Curl paper strips to make wild hair. Glue the head in place around the short ends of the straws.

4. Stick a toothpick between the taped ends.

5. Adjust the length and the angle of the long ends of the straw so that the alien balances on your fingertip. Then, try balancing the alien on the tightrope described on page 71.

A Fine Balance

How'd That Happen?

Try to balance a book on its corner. Difficult, isn't it? Can you guess what's supporting the weight of the book? The support base (the corner) is very small and the book's center of gravity is too far above it.

Now try placing a book on its edge. Is it harder to knock over? True, it's less wobbly, but the center of gravity is still too high and the support (the edge) is too narrow.

Finally, place a book on a table as you normally would. Push that book all around. No wobble now! A book's most stable position is flat on the table. The support base is large and the book's center of gravity is down low.

Laying an object like a book on a table won't impress anyone. But balancing an alien on a tiny support (the toothpick) is impressive because it's not what our experience tells us is correct. But because the gizmo's center of gravity is down low and evenly distributed, this bizarre-looking gizmo balances just fine!

Science Clues

What does the center of gravity have to do with spinners? See page 102.

Whose Bright Idea?

MARY ANDERSON

Stop the Drip-Drop

Carrots, cardboard tubes, and forks might seem like strange materials for concocting a balancing toy. But many of our most helpful inventions got their start when someone thought of a new use for everyday things. Such was the case in 1903. Mary Anderson was fed up with rainy-day trolley car rides. Did the driver really have to get out at every block to wipe the windows? There must be a better way!

Back home, problem-solver Anderson got to work. She experimented with the sponges and sticks she had on hand. Rubber on poles was her final design. These wipers could be attached to the outside of the window, but controlled by the driver from the inside.

Since then, other inventors have improved the design. Automatic, variable-speed windshield wipers sure had a strange start!

Fun, Fab Balancing Lab

Scrounge around your home for odds and ends. Try balancing combinations of whatever you have on hand: cereal box cardboard, cardboard tubes, corks; carrots, potatoes, fruit; pennies, washers, paper clips; toothpicks, straws, plastic or metal forks, chopsticks, pencils. Find it, then try it!

The Rules of Balance
Remember these tips as you create crazy balancing contraptions:

- An object balances when the support point is in line with the object's center of gravity. The support (like your finger) must be directly on, above, or below the center of gravity.
- The object is most stable (in balance) when the center of gravity is down low.

SUPER BIRD This bird balances only by its beak!

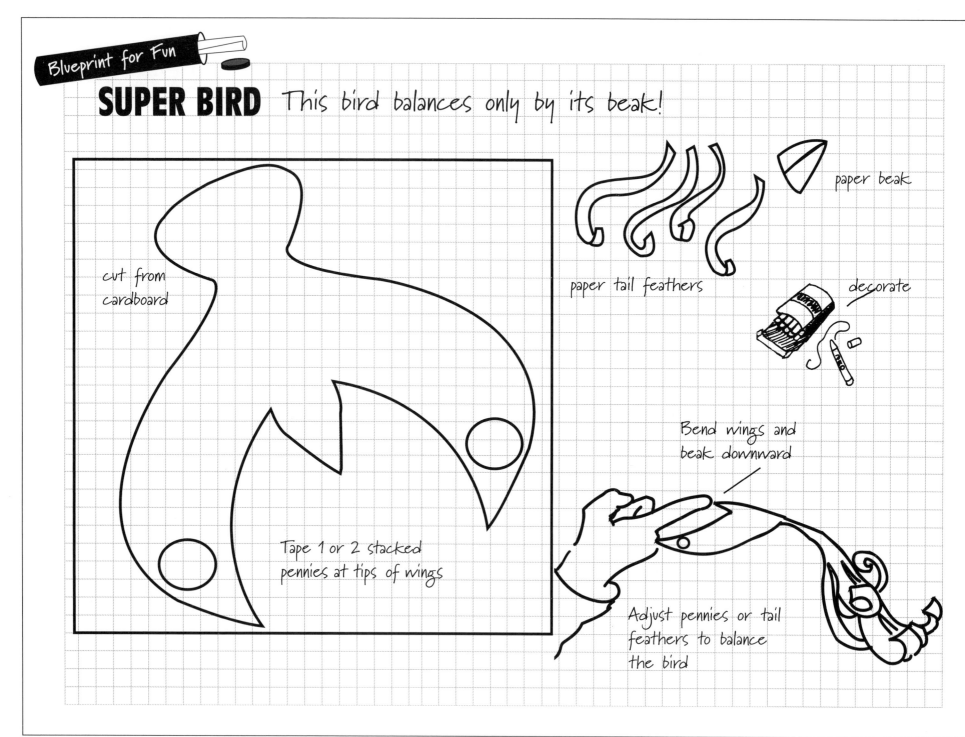

cut from cardboard

paper tail feathers

paper beak

decorate

Tape 1 or 2 stacked pennies at tips of wings

Bend wings and beak downward

Adjust pennies or tail feathers to balance the bird

ON THE HIGH WIRE

◎ Who is the more talented tightrope walker, one who uses a pole, or one who does not?

◎ Which bus is more stable, a single or a double decker? A short bus is, but the double decker is so much more fun to ride! Is there anything an engineer can do to keep this giant from toppling over? For the double-decker bus, how about placing heavy parts like the engine down low and having a nice wide wheel track width?

DOWNTOWN

Answer: *The one with no pole. Without a pole, there's less weight to shift easily when you're out of balance.*

Imagine you're at the circus, and the high-wire act has just begun. Out steps a tightrope walker. Now that you know more about balance, can you guess why she's carrying a long pole? (It's the same reason you thrust your arms out to the sides when you walk along the top of a low wall.)

As the tightrope walker shifts her weight from side to side, the pole counteracts that shift of weight, so she can keep her overall center of gravity over the wire, and stay in balance! A curved pole is best. With the ends pointing downward, the center of gravity is lowered, giving the walker even more stability.

Spill Thrills!

This monster rocks back and forth as you add weight to his arms. Keep him in balance, or he'll spill his load and be furious!

Let's build it!

1. Cut the plastic lid in half. Center a small cardboard tube between the halves. Staple them in place so that they act as rockers.

2. Punch holes in either side of the cardboard tube. Poke a pencil through the holes to act as arms. Check to see that the gizmo balances so that the roll stands upright. Readjust the staples if needed.

3. Decorate the roll to look like a monster, using marking pens and colorful scraps of paper.

4. You and a friend each need a pile of plastic bag locking tabs. Take turns rolling a die. On your turn, place the number of tabs rolled onto the arms of the monster. You may put some or all of the tabs on either arm. The trick is to place the tabs so that the monster doesn't tip over and spill the tabs. If the monster loses its balance, you lose, too!

Tools & Supplies

- ◎ Large plastic lid
- ◎ Scissors
- ◎ Cardboard tube
- ◎ Stapler
- ◎ Hole punch
- ◎ Pencil, chopstick, or dowel
- ◎ Colored markers
- ◎ Paper scraps
- ◎ Plastic bag locking tabs (found on bread bags or in grocery stores)
- ◎ Tape
- ◎ Dice

Get Even

Putting tabs on one arm adds weight to that side, pulling it downward. Adding tabs to the opposite side, at just the right places, balances the weight on the first arm. When the arms are level and the gizmo sits still, it's in balance.

Alligator Rock

Cut a paper plate in half. Glue a small box between the halves to separate them so that they work like rockers. Now for the creative fun! Glue on cardboard shapes to transform the rocker into a moving critter, like the alligator shown here. Use metal paper fasteners to attach moving parts such as the ears, legs, tail, or jaws.

Messing Around

Whose Bright Idea?

ALEXIA ABERNATHY

Imagine a little kid's messy meal as the inspiration for a balanced invention. It was for Alexia Abernathy. Although her Oops! Proof No-Spill Bowl didn't win the school's invention contest, it *did* win the interest of Little Kids, Inc. Being a kid was an advantage. Alexia's "Hello, I'm a fifth grader" letter describing her invention really caught the company's attention, and a new kind of bowl was born!

Fast Physics

Seesaw Fun

Experiment with balance on a seesaw, with a friend.

◎ Sit so that the seesaw goes back and forth evenly.
◎ What makes one friend get stuck high in the air?
◎ Balance a lightweight kid with a heavier friend.

It's not just *how much* weight is placed on each arm that determines balance; it's also *where* that weight is placed. *The closer a heavy weight is to the center of the seesaw, the farther from the center the lighter weight must be for the seesaw to be in balance.*

Whose Bright Idea?

ALEXANDER CALDER

ART IN BALANCE

Alexander Calder was an artist who studied engineering. He creatively combined his love for both physics and art and perfected the mobile — a unique masterpiece that moved! Calder, inspired by the solar system, said, "I work from a large, live model!"

Try this: Use red, white, blue, yellow, and black shapes (Calder's favorite colors) and any odds and ends you have on hand (his studio looked like a recycling center!) to make a Calder-style mobile.

Face It!

Put balance in beautiful motion by making an artistic mobile! It's as easy to balance a symmetrical (see page 71) mobile as it is to balance a seesaw. What hangs from each side is exactly the same. Make a funny-face mobile by using thread to attach eye and ear shapes near the ends of a coat hanger. Add nose and mouth shapes right down the center. Now, ask a grown-up to help you hang the mobile from the ceiling and watch it dance in the breeze!

Hee Hee..

We did it!

!? Have you ever spun around so much you felt dizzy? Would you believe it's because of your ears? Your inner ear contains a special fluid that moves as you move your head. Spinning disturbs the balance of the fluid so you end up feeling off balance, too!

THE EYES HAVE IT

Time how long you can stand on one foot. Now, time yourself again, standing on one foot with your eyes closed. You just lost an important sensory clue your body needs to balance. Prepare to fall in no time at all!

The Spin on Things

What helps a washing machine wring water out of wet clothes and makes a boomerang return to you? Spinning motion! From eggbeaters to water whirling down the tub drain to a day on planet Earth, spinning motion is everywhere! If you think going in circles is cool, give these spinning gizmos a whirl.

Go on a spin search. Look for all sorts of things that spin around your home — indoors and out, manmade and created by nature. Are you getting the spin on things?

Super Spinners!

Experiment to make a super-duper top!

Tools & Supplies
◎ Jar lid, old CD, or other round shape
◎ Pencils
◎ Cereal box cardboard
◎ Scissors
◎ Rubber bands

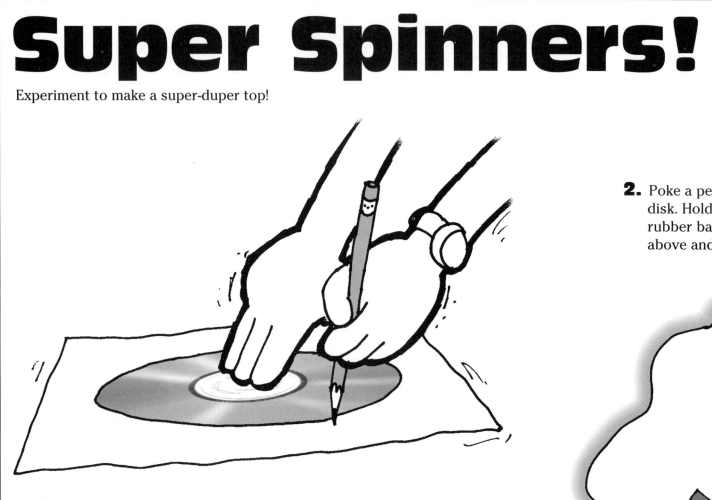

2. Poke a pencil through a cardboard disk. Hold it firmly in place by winding rubber bands tightly around the pencil above and below the cardboard.

Let's build it!

A cardboard disk makes a base for a top. A pencil forms a tip and handle. Combine them in different ways to build tester tops.

1. Draw several circles on cardboard by tracing around a lid or an old CD. Cut them out.

Testing, Testing

◎ Spin a pencil on its point. Spin a cardboard disk. What happens?

◎ Poke the pencil through a disk at a point away from the center. How's the motion?

◎ Give your spinner a long handle and a short tip by pushing just a little of the pencil through the hole. How's the spinning action?

◎ Now push most of a pencil through a cardboard circle to make a long-tipped spinner with a short handle. Does the spin change?

◎ Spin a square or triangle shape cut from cardboard. Poke a pencil through the center, and give it a whirl.

Which top stays spinning for the longest time?

"Pay" for a Better Spin

Want to improve the spin? Tape six pennies onto the rim of one cardboard disk. On another disk, tape six pennies close to the center. Poke pencils through both disks and set them spinning. Compare the wobbles.

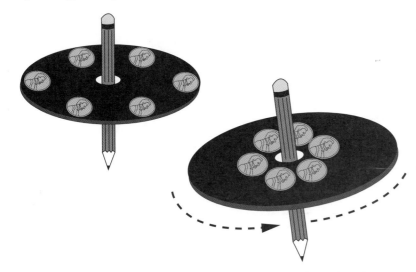

The neat thing about spinning things like tops is that they keep on spinning, long after you've set them in motion! Why? *Rotational inertia* is at work. (To rotate means to spin; see pages 9-12 for more on inertia.) More mass (weight) placed at the outer edge of a spinning object, like the top, increases its inertia, achieving an even better spin!

!? Looking for the longest ride? Where is the best place for you and your friends to sit on a playground merry-go-round, at the edge or near the center?

Answer: At the edge, to improve the spinning inertia.

May the Best Top Win!

Put your best design features together to produce a super spin.

1. Space eight pennies or washers equal distances apart along the outside edge of a cardboard circle. Glue them in place. Add a dab of glue to the top of each penny; then, place another cardboard circle on top so that you've made a penny sandwich. Place under heavy books and let dry overnight.

HEY!

GLUE

2. Poke a pencil through the exact center of the cardboard circle. Be sure the handle is long and the tip is short. Hold in place with rubber bands as shown.

3. Add a cardboard-tube handle (see "Terrific Torque," page 94).

4. Give your super spinner a whirl. Compare the action with the tester tops (page 91). Does your super spinner beat them all?

Terrific Torque

Want to speed up the spin? Cut a section from a toilet-paper tube. Punch holes through the top and bottom. Drop it over the pencil handle of your top. (The handle should be able to turn freely.) Hold the cardboard as you wind about 2 feet (60 cm) of cord around the pencil handle. To launch, hold the cardboard as you pull quickly on the cord.

Be sure this turns freely

Science Speak!

Torque (TORK) is the force you add to make something rotate (spin). When you twist the handle of a top or pull a string to get it going, you're adding torque, making it spin faster.

Fast Physics

Pedal Power!

Go for a bike ride to get a feel for spinning power. The faster you pedal and get those wheels spinning, the harder you must push on the brakes to stop. Spinning things are hard to stop! **Once spinning, they keep spinning until stopped by another force.**

Pedal hard again. Now stop pedaling, but don't apply the brakes. You'd coast on forever if it weren't for friction slowing you down and gravity pulling you over. Imagine *that* ride!

Winner Spinner

How'd That Happen?

What design features make a top-notch top?

◎ **A disk** evenly distributes the mass about the center. That's also why poking the pencil through the very center works best.

◎ **A long handle and a short tip.** The top is more stable when it has a low center of gravity.

◎ **Weight evenly distributed at the outer edge** gives the top more spinning inertia.

◎ **The greater the torque,** the longer the spin.

SPINNERS GALORE!

Now that you've got spinning figured out, devise your own spinning creations, using lids, plates, cardboard, and other scrounged materials. Which designs work the best?

Top Tracks

Check out the tracks your spinning top leaves! Push a thin felt-tipped marker through a hole in the center of a 1-quart (1-L) yogurt container lid. Set the top on a piece of paper. Now spin it. What pattern does it make? Use different-colored pens to make more designs.

!? Imagine a top so massive, it can spin for almost an hour and a half! Well, in 1986, 25 people set a top spinning that measured $6^1/2$ feet (2 m) high and $8^1/2$ feet (2.6 m) wide. It weighed almost 800 pounds (363 kg)! Lots of mass equals longtime motion.

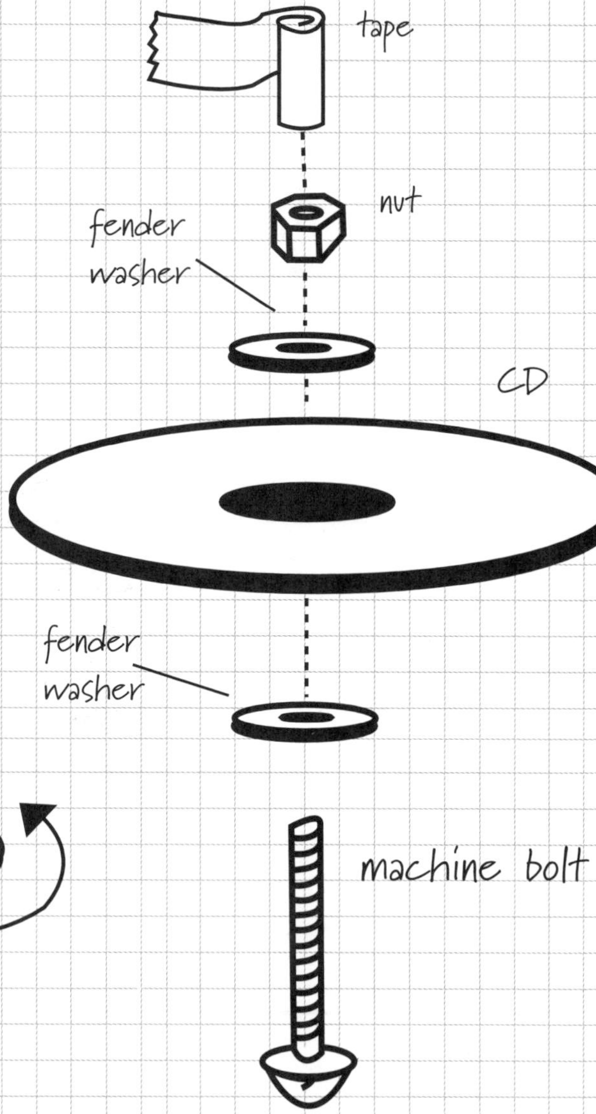

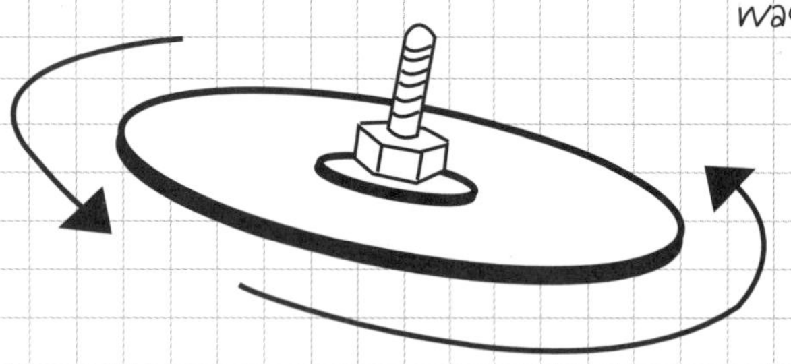

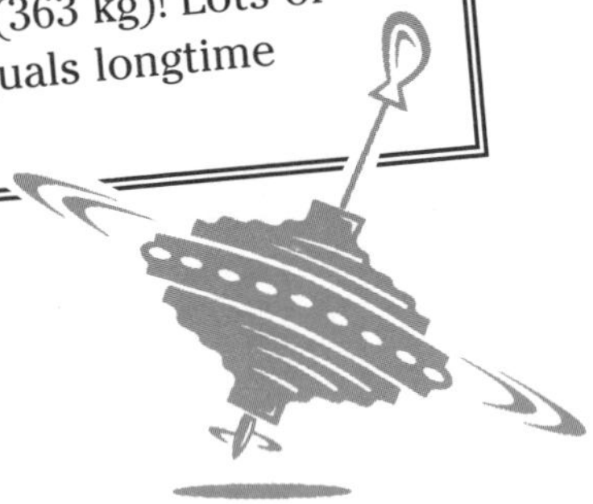

Blueprint for Fun

THE CD SPECIAL

Spin this top in the sunlight to create a light show on your walls!

tape
nut
fender washer
CD
fender washer
machine bolt

Science Clues

Learn about the top-stopping forces of *friction* and *gravity*. **See pages 28 and 49.**

Dinky Rink

Can the spin of these tiny tops defy gravity?

Let's build it!

Construct the rink

Cut a large circle, about 18 inches (45 cm) across, from poster board. Make a slit from the outer edge to the center of the circle. Overlap the edge by about an inch (2.5 cm) and secure with strips of tape on both sides of the cone. Set the pointed end of the cone in a bowl.

Tools & Supplies
- ◎ Scissors
- ◎ Poster board
- ◎ Tape
- ◎ Small bowl
- ◎ Round toothpicks
- ◎ Egg carton
- ◎ Milk jug cap
- ◎ Pushpin
- ◎ Smooth-edged lid from a 12-oz. (375-ml) frozen orange juice container
- ◎ Pencil
- ◎ Cereal box cardboard

Build the tops

Poke a toothpick through each type of base.

◎ **Egg carton.** Cut out a section and trim the bottom edge so it's even.

◎ **Cardboard circle.** Trace around the smooth-edged lid of a frozen orange juice container for just the right size.

◎ **Milk jug cap**. Use a pushpin to start the hole in the center.

Spin the tops by twisting them and then letting them go over the rink. Which design stays up the longest?

Mini Yo-Yo Magic

Can you think of another gravity-defying spinner? The yo-yo is one! Here's a mini yo-yo you can make yourself.

Connect two identical buttons by holding them flat-sides together and stitching thread back and forth several times through the holes. Knot the thread on the outside of the buttons to secure. Tie one end of about 24 inches (60 cm) of thread to the threads you just stitched between the buttons. Wind this thread tightly, as you would the string of a larger yo-yo. Make a loop for your finger at the end. Then, get the yo-yo spinning by moving your hand up and down.

Take a Turn

How'd That Happen?

Spinning objects can get going so fast, with so much rotational inertia, that they defy gravity!

Whose Bright Idea?

DONALD DUNCAN

Duncan Knew!

We think of the yo-yo as a plastic or wooden modern-day toy, but actually, yo-yos have been around for thousands of years! Kids in ancient Egypt, Greece, and China enjoyed the ups and downs of yo-yos, too.

What's new about yo-yos is marketing. Someone with a creative mind can take a product from one place and introduce it to another. That's just what businessman Donald Duncan did in 1920. He wondered, "Would American children enjoy spinning these spinning gadgets?" The millions of Duncan yo-yos that have been sold since sure have answered his question!

!? How do you launch an 897-pound (408-kg) yo-yo? From a crane! That's just what college students did in Wyenshawe, England, in 1993. It spun up and down four times!

How'd That Happen?

Yo!

Yo!

The Ups and Downs

Your tugging force gets the yo-yo spinning. Friction and the yo-yo's special design create that awesome up-and-down motion.

Boomerangs

Tired of chasing a ball when none of your friends can play? Try throwing a boomerang. The special shape of this gizmo causes it to come back full circle, returning to you — thanks to the laws of physics!

Let's build it!

1. Sketch two of the same kind of arm onto cardboard. Cut them out. Use rubber bands to connect the arms.

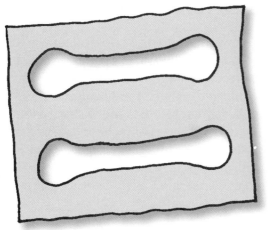

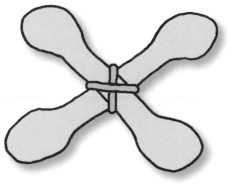

2. Fling your boomerang parallel to the ground like a Frisbee, or hold it vertical to the ground and snap your wrist as you release it.

Design Your Own!

Even more fun than tossing a boomerang is tinkering with the design. Make boomerangs with one, two, or three arms. Which works best? Now, create your own arm design.

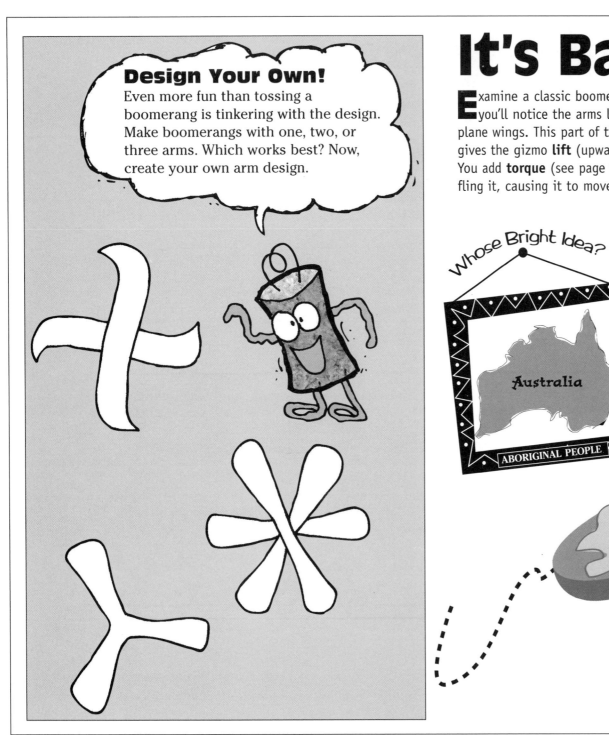

It's Back!

How'd That Happen?

Examine a classic boomerang and you'll notice the arms look like airplane wings. This part of the design gives the gizmo **lift** (upward force). You add **torque** (see page 94) as you fling it, causing it to move like a top in the air. A boomerang spins rapidly away from the thrower until **drag**, or air friction (see page 43), slows it down. Its special shape causes it to move in a circular path back to its starting point — you!

Whose Bright Idea?

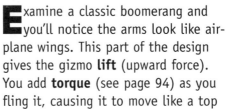

Australia

ABORIGINAL PEOPLE

The Way It Was . . .

Centuries ago, the boomerang wasn't a plaything; It was a serious wooden hunting weapon. Credit for the clever design goes to the Aboriginal people of Australia. It took a lot of experimenting with different objects to get just the right size, weight, and shape — just like your tests to create a come-back cardboard version.

!? How is a boomerang like a bagel? They both have their centers of gravity (see page 76) outside their bodies. For the bagel, it's right in the hole. For the boomerang, it's the point it spins about when hurled by you!

Fling-a-ma-jigs

Tools & Supplies
◎ Paper plates
◎ Scissors
◎ White glue

When is a pie plate not a pie plate? When it's a Frisbee! In honor of the Frisbee's creative beginnings (see page 104), use paper plates for your models of the famous Frisbee and Aerobie flyers.

Let's build it!

Frisbee-Style

Cut out the bottom of one paper plate. Glue along the inside edge. Press another *uncut* paper plate against the edge. Press together to seal.

Aerobie-Style

Cut the bottoms from three paper plates. Glue together one layer at a time. Test the action before adding each layer.

HURRY UP!

Fling each of these gizmos just as you would a classic Frisbee.

Fast Physics

Circle Game

Lay the edge of a jar lid over your pencil eraser. Now, move the pencil in small circles. What happens to the lid? Suddenly, it's no longer drooping downward; it's spinning parallel to the ground. The spinning lid pulls outward with enough force to keep it upright, fighting gravity — like the Frisbee and the Aerobie!

PIE-PAN PLAY

Whose Bright Idea?

WALTER MORRISON

!? The amazing Aerobie has been known to fly more than 1,000 feet (308 km) in a single fling — that's farther than the length of a football field!

FRISBIE!

BONK!

There was only one thing college students liked better than eating pies from the Frisbie Pie Company. That was tossing the empty metal pans back and forth! They'd shout, "Frisbie!" to warn others of their discus throwing.

The game inspired Walter Morrison to look at something old in a new way to create a totally different (and fun!) product. In the 1950s, he took his idea to the Wham-O Manufacturing Company. The company experimented with materials to find something light enough for safety, yet heavy enough to fly. Soft, tough plastic was the answer. The name Frisbee, with only a slight spelling change, stuck to the popular flyer we fling today.

Then along came Alan Adler. Like many great inventors, he was determined to create the best possible design. He realized that if he could reduce the Frisbee's drag, he would create a gizmo that could travel even farther. Persistence paid off. After years of tinkering he came up with a specially crafted ring — the Aerobie — that outdistanced the Frisbee.

THINK CREATIVELY!

Inventors are very creative. They combine knowledge with materials in a way no one has ever done before to create something totally new and useful. Inventors are able to see beyond the way things have always been done. A pie plate holds pies. Right? It's not a toy you toss across a field to your friend. Or is it? As an inventor, your challenge is to look at what's common in an uncommon way. With creative thinking, anything is possible!

When in a Pinch...

Thank goodness these inventive cooks took a chance with creative solutions!

◎ **Chocolate Chip Cookies.** With no melting chocolate on hand, baker Ruth Wakefield stirred broken chocolate candy bar pieces into her batter. She expected them to melt into swirls. But to the delight of her customers, they remained softened chunks of chocolate. It all happened back in 1930 at the Toll House Inn in New Bedford, Massachusetts. Chocolate chip cookies, anyone?

YAY!

◎ **Ice-Cream Cones.** It was a hot day at the 1904 World's Fair (as the story goes) and ice-cream vendor Charles Menches had a problem. No more serving dishes! But the waffle vendor had an idea. He rolled up his waffles into cones. Yum! Much tastier than a dish!

Weird Whirlers

Surprise your friends with these wacky gizmos.

Swing-a-Ma-Jig

Turn a cup of water upside down over your head and you'll get soaked, right? Take a chance and see for yourself.

1. Poke three holes, evenly spaced around the top, in a tall, clear plastic deli container.

2. Thread about 10 inches (25 cm) of cord through each hole. Tie a knot at each hole to secure the cord in place; then, knot the three cords together at the loose ends.

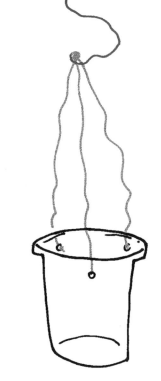

3. Attach about a yard (1 m) of cord where the three cords meet. Be sure all knots are tight and will hold!

Tools & Supplies
◎ Plastic deli containers
◎ Cord or string
◎ Carrot
◎ Large thread spool or toilet-paper tube
◎ Eraser
◎ Ping-Pong ball

4. Now, fill the container half full of water. Go outdoors and start swinging the gizmo by the long cord. When you feel confident, swing the water around in a huge circle, over your head.

Are you still dry?

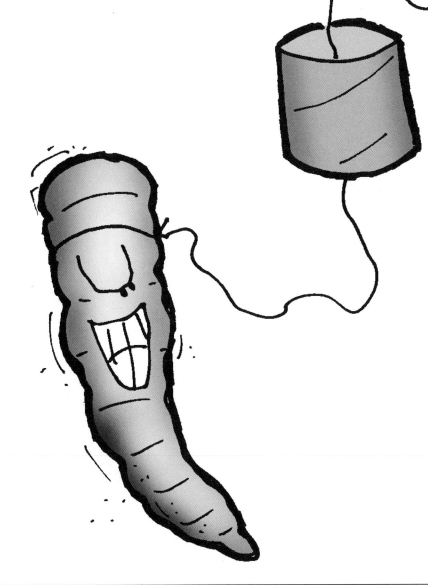

Spin Lifter

Which object would you bet on to win at tug-of-war, an eraser or a carrot? Check your prediction against this gizmo.

Tie about a yard (1 m) of string to the top of a carrot. Slip the other end through a large thread spool or toilet-paper tube; then, tie it to an eraser. Move the spool in a circle, and try to get the eraser spinning.
What happens to the carrot?

Ping-Pong Orbiter

Have a grown-up cut the bottom from a deli container. Set the container over a Ping-Pong ball. Rotate the container with one hand to get the ball rolling inside as fast as possible. Can you lift the ball off the table and keep it from falling without touching the ball?

What's Goin' Round?

Congratulations! You just created a powerful **centripetal force** in each of these weird whirlers. Nothing can travel in a circle without centripetal force, and in these cases, that force came from you! The faster the whirl, the greater the force. Can you see why the weird whirlers move the way they do?

◎ The spinning eraser tugs outward with enough force to lift an object much heavier than itself — the carrot. If you placed your bets on the lightweight contender, you won!

◎ The spinning water tries to travel outward in a straight line, following Newton's first law (see page 10) so it pushes against the walls of the container, defying gravity's downward pull. No water spills! But when the spinning stops, watch out below!

◎ The spinning Ping-Pong ball tries to fly outward in a straight line, too. *Wham!* It hits the wall of the container, where it circles around, defying the downward pull of gravity ... until the spinning stops.

Science Speak!

Centripetal force is the force that keeps an object moving in a circle. Nothing can travel in a circle without centripetal force.

Join the Whirl!

Feel physics in your fist by tying an eraser onto about a yard (1 m) of string and then giving it a whirl. Where does the eraser go? Do you feel the tug through the string?

◎ Twirl the string fast, then slow. Notice the difference.
◎ Stop twirling. What happens to the eraser?
◎ Let go of the string after you've got it whirling.

May the force (centripetal force, that is) be with you!

Feel the tug of the eraser as it whirls around? Let go and the force is gone! The eraser soars off in a straight line following Newton's first law of motion (good old inertia again). Stop your spin and the eraser drops, no longer defying gravity.

!? Have you ever been turned completely upside down on a roller coaster ride? You didn't fall out, of course. Roller coaster cars go up and over in a huge circle, yet the screaming riders stay aboard. Bet you know why now!

Lost in Space (Not!)

Centripetal force is a very powerful force; it's so powerful that it even keeps satellites spinning in space! Imagine Earth's gravity (the string), pulling on a satellite (the eraser). It places a centripetal force on the satellite, keeping it spinning around Earth instead of flying out in a straight path through outer space. If the satellite slows down, the force of gravity takes over and pulls it back to Earth. So, you just made a model showing how a satellite stays in orbit. It's centripetal force at work!

Fast Physics

Watch That Curve!

SPLAT!

Have you noticed how your body leans sideways in a car as you round a bend in the road? That tug you feel is caused by **inertia.** (It's the same force that tugs on the water, the eraser, and the Ping-Pong ball when they're on a weird whirl.) Your body, set in motion, tries to move in a straight line, while the car is turning the bend. The faster the object travels (the car with you in it), the stronger the outward movement. It's a good thing your car has sides and seat belts!

Spectacular Swirl Art

Set a circle of paper or a small paper plate in the bottom of an old salad spinner. Spoon different colors of liquid tempera paints onto the paper, replace the lid, and spin. As a spin expert, can you tell what made the paint fly?

And in the Winner's Circle...

Athletes understand centripetal force. The hammer thrower applies force to whirl a weight in a circle. When the athlete lets go, the force is gone so the hammer flies off in a straight line, following its inertia. The faster the thrower spins the weight, the farther the released hammer travels. Physics and physical strength win the competition!

Energize!

Energy makes things happen! We use energy to microwave a snack, surf the Internet, and get moving on a skateboard, and we try to save it by turning off lights when we don't need them. We energize ourselves by eating foods like apples, French fries, and even "energy" bars. And when we're on the go, people say, "You've got a lot of energy!"

But what is **energy?** What does it really do? Find out as you build action-packed gadgets that hurl, spin, swing, and make things happen. Get energized!

Merry-Go-Round

How much energy can a simple rubber band deliver? Use a few to power a merry-go-round and find out!

Let's build it!

The motor

1. With a grown-up's help, poke holes in the center of the soda bottle cap and base.

2. Make a rubber-band chain about the same length as the bottle (loop two or three bands together).

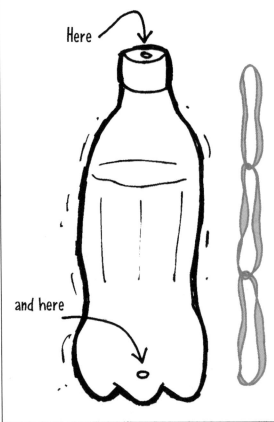

Here

and here

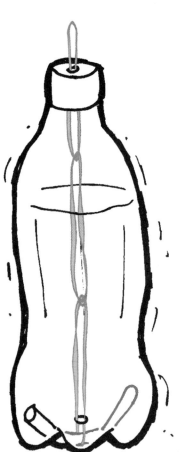

3. Thread the rubber-band chain through the hole in the base of the bottle. Secure it by catching a short piece of drinking straw through the last rubber-band loop. Set the straw in the indent at the base of the bottle and tape it securely in place.

Tools & Supplies
◎ Small plastic soda bottle with cap
◎ Rubber bands
◎ Plastic drinking straw
◎ Tape
◎ Jumbo paper clip
◎ Washer
◎ Pencil or chopstick
◎ Dried beans
◎ Paper
◎ Scissors
◎ Thread

4. Make a hook with the paper clip to pull the other end of the rubber-band chain through the hole in the cap and through the washer. Secure the cap. Catch the loop at the top of the band with the pencil or chopstick.

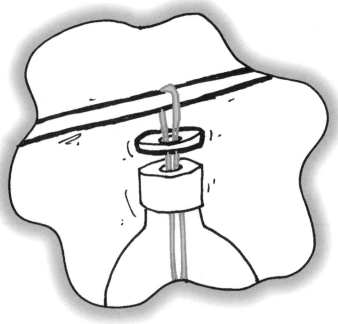

The merry-go-round

1. Draw birds on paper like the ones shown and cut them out. Wind thread around the tip of the pencil or chopstick and dangle a bird from each side.

2. Center the pencil or chopstick on the cap of the bottle and wind it up. What do you predict will happen when you let go?

5. Untwist the cap and pull it away from the opening far enough so that you and a friend can fill the bottle with a couple of inches (about 5 cm) of dried beans. Use just enough to make the container stand steady.

Science Clues

What happens to the birds as the Merry-Go-Round spins? (See page 108.)

It's a Motor!

How'd That Happen?

By winding the rubber band and forcing it into a twisted shape, you stored energy in it. Releasing the pencil or chopstick got things happening. As the band returned to its original shape, the energy came back out as motion — a motion strong enough to power a merry-go-round! Bravo! You just created a rubber-band motor!

Science Speak!

Energy makes things happen. Scientists define energy as *the ability to cause change* — like the movement of a merry-go-round.

Fast Physics

TA DA...

RUBBER-BAND POWER

What's so powerful about a rubber band? Stretch one out and aim for a wall. At the moment the rubber band is stretched, it's packed with stored energy. Just think of all that potential! Release the band, and what happens? (No folks or pets in the flight path, please!) It's flying, as stored energy changes to moving energy!

!? Every gizmo in this book moves. So does every gizmo shown use energy?

Answer: Yes.

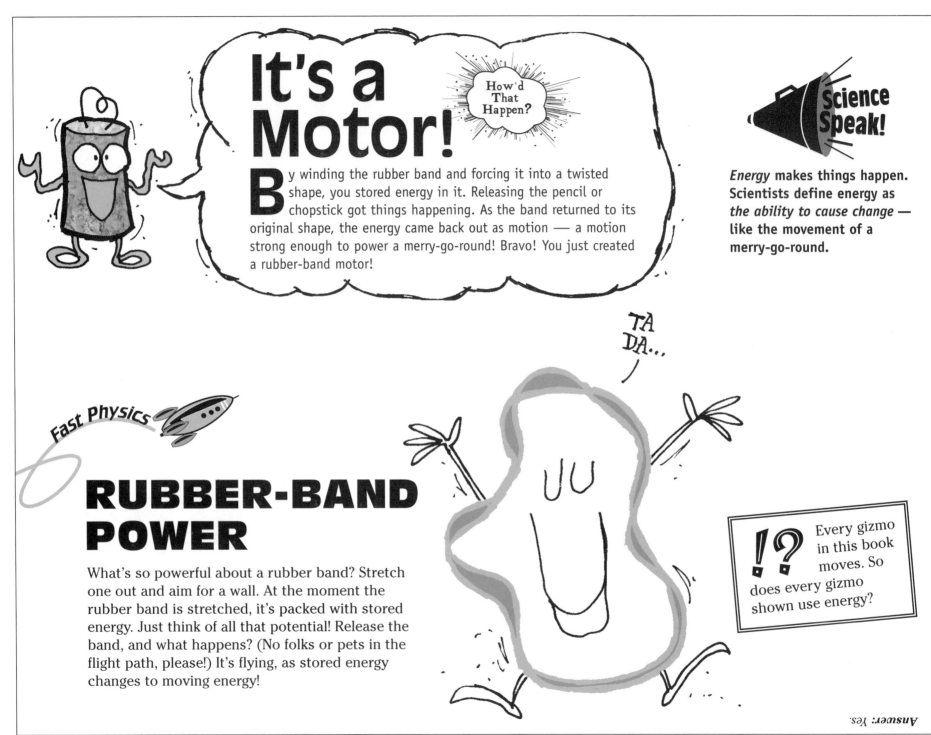

It's Got Potential!

What do a rock at the tip of a mountaintop, a stretched slingshot, and a match all have in common? If you're thinking each of them has potential, you're right — **potential energy,** that is! It's the energy that's stored and ready to change to **kinetic energy**, or moving energy.

◎ The slingshot has potential energy because it's stretched out and ready to snap back into its relaxed shape (just like the Merry-Go-Round).

◎ The rock has potential energy because gravity is ready to pull it down toward the earth (like the Marble Ramp on page 59).

◎ The match has potential because of what it's made of. Strike it, and the energy stored in the chemicals at the tip changes to heat energy. (See "More Power to You!" on page 21.)

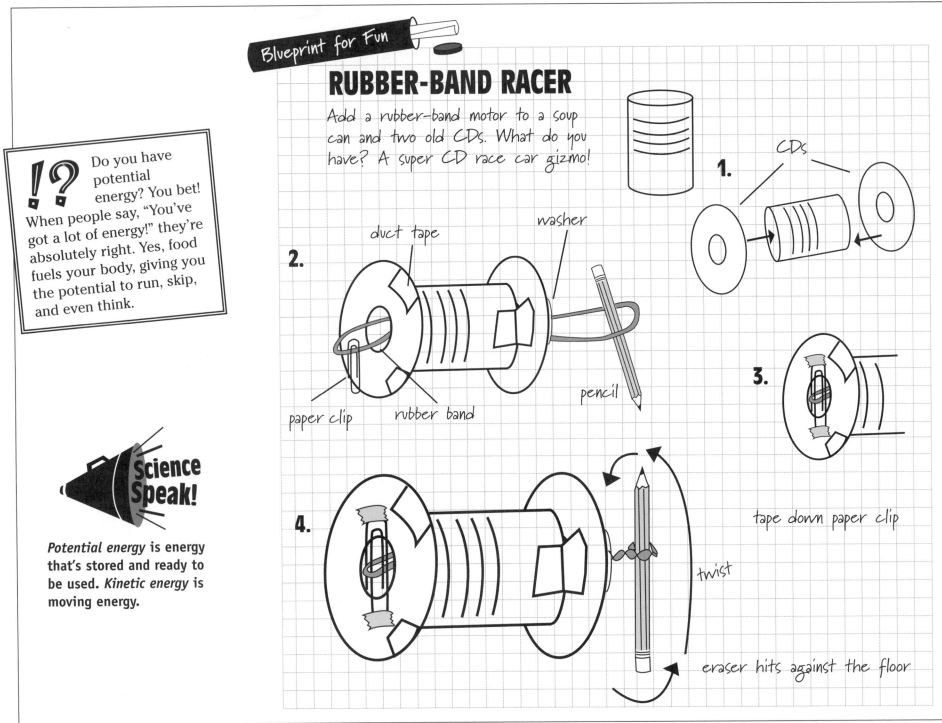

RUBBER-BAND RACER

Add a rubber-band motor to a soup can and two old CDs. What do you have? A super CD race car gizmo!

1. CDs

2. duct tape washer

paper clip rubber band pencil

3. tape down paper clip

4. twist

eraser hits against the floor

Rev It Up!

Create the perfect racer and decorate it with markers or paint. Then, race it against your friend's best design.

Improve the Design

- Try a plastic vitamin bottle, a toilet-paper tube, or an oatmeal box. Poke holes at each end.
- Experiment with paper plates, lids, or no wheels at all.
- Try a pencil, chopstick, or knitting needle.

Maximize the Power

Use a thick, thin, doubled, or a few rubber bands looped together.

Improve the Spin

Add a washer. Rub soap or candle wax on the place where the arm rubs to reduce friction.

Scary Surprises

Rattle, Rattle, Rattle-Mouth

Pack energy into a rubber band. Then, sit back and listen to the racket!

1. Cut a square hole from the front panel of a small cardboard box, right where you want the monster's mouth to be.

2. Glue construction paper over the outside of the box, covering everything but the square mouth. Use paper scraps and markers to decorate it to look like a monster's head.

3. Color the flap of cardboard you removed from the hole to look like a tongue. Trim it so that it can turn in the mouth hole, but will still catch lightly on an edge as it spins.

4. Stretch two rubber bands around the box, centered over the mouth opening. Place the tongue flap between the rubber bands and twist it about 20 times. Wait for just the right moment; then, let go!

BRRAAAAAAP!

Rattlesnake Scare

Something handy about energy is that you can save it for later use — such as when you're ready to surprise a friend!

1. Create the gizmo shown with a re-bent jumbo paper clip, washer, and two small rubber bands. Tape it to the center of a 5-inch x 12-inch (12.5-cm x 30-cm) strip of cardboard, and fold the cardboard into thirds. On the cover, write, "Contents: Baby rattlesnake eggs. Caution! Eggs may hatch if exposed to light!"

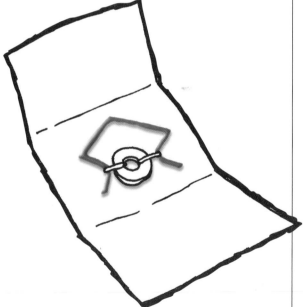

2. Wind the washer many times. Close the cardboard flaps and hold in place with a paper clip. Then, hand the package to a curious friend or two, and watch their surprise as they open it!

Whose Bright Idea?

LUIGI GALVANI

Whose Bright Idea?

ALESSANDRO VOLTA

It's a Kick!

What does every household have in many places, storing lots and lots of energy? That's right, batteries! You can find them in everything from your family car to your favorite action toy. A questioning mind contributed to *this* bright idea.

It was a frog leg that got Luigi Galvani thinking more than 200 years ago. Amazingly, it twitched when he touched it with two different metals. The frog must hold electricity, he thought.

Not so, said Alessandro Volta. He questioned the results of Galvani's experiment and set up his own. (He knew that things aren't always what they seem.) Volta was able to prove that it was the metals that caused the electricity, not the frog's leg. His first battery was an acid-soaked pad stored between two pieces of metal.

Since then, inventors have experimented with many different metals and acids to make the super-efficient batteries we depend on today.

Ribbit!

Marshmallow Catapult

What's more fun than flinging marshmallows into the air?
Making the contraption that sends them flying!

Tools & Supplies
◎ Two 1-quart (1-L) plastic
   soda bottles
◎ 2 pencils
◎ 3 rubber bands
◎ Scissors
◎ Hole punch
◎ Tape
◎ Index card or small box
◎ Dried beans
◎ Marshmallows

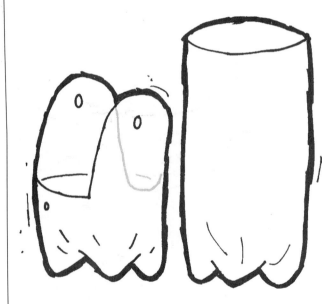

Let's build it!

1. With a grown-up's help, cut the tops off two plastic soda bottles, and cut the bottoms into the shapes shown.

2. Punch three holes in the smaller section as shown. Poke a pencil through the two side holes.

3. Loop a rubber band through the bottom hole. Catch a pencil through the loop. Twist other rubber bands on either side of the loop to hold it in place. Place this pencil across the other pencil, and secure them to each other with rubber bands as shown.

4. Create a marshmallow holder by folding and taping the sides of an index card into a lid shape (or use a small box). Tape the holder to the top of the pencil so that the tip sticks out.

5. Fill the large bottom section of the bottle with beans to stabilize the catapult. Jam the other section into the weighted bottom.

6. Place a marshmallow in the holder. Push down on the pencil tip while holding onto the base. Then release it, and watch it fly! (Caution: Launch only marshmallows!)

Handy Pocket Flinger

Use two rubber bands to attach the handle of a plastic spoon to a small block of wood. Place a marshmallow in the cup of the spoon. Press, release, and watch the action!

Ammo

Heads Up!

Catapults have sent stuff flying for thousands of years. The first catapult may have simply been a young tree bent back and then released. The Romans improved the design with stretchy cord made from twisted hair or dried animal tendons.

Medieval engineers designed catapult contraptions that could throw 300-pound (136-kg) boulders! Some designs were so massive they sat on wheeled platforms with hefty weights holding down the heavy arm. Cutting the weights free flung a variety of interesting and disgusting stuff through the air: rocks, arrows, burning straw, dead animals, dung, even the heads of enemies. Yuck!

What makes an arrow travel fast and far? The bow! Think about its shape when it's drawn. There's energy stored in both the wood and the cord as they're pulled away from each other. Release them, and both spring back to their original shapes. Energy is passed on to the arrow, propelling it at great speed over a long distance.
Bull's-eye!

Design Your Own Catapult

As long as you have an *arm to hurl* the marshmallows, *elastic material* to store and release energy, and *a base or way to hold* the contraption in place, you can set a marshmallow flying!

Up, Up, & Away

How'd That Happen?

This catapult is energized like the Merry-Go-Round (page 112). Stretching, like twisting, builds up energy in the band. The stored (potential) energy changes into moving (kinetic) energy as the stretched band springs back into shape with enough force to fling the marshmallow through the air.

Because the force is transferred to the marshmallow, the flying marshmallow now has kinetic energy!

Fast Physics

Fantastic Elastic

You know that when stretchy stuff — like a rubber band — is pulled out of shape, it tries to get back into shape. As it changes back, it moves, so energy is released.

A trampoline is elastic, or stretchy, too. Your heavy, bouncing body is the force that makes a trampoline stretch out of shape. As the trampoline moves back to its original shape, it pushes back against you. The result? You bounce even higher into the air! When you hit the trampoline, the stretching, pushing action starts all over again.

Pendulum Pal

Make your own superhero sail through the sky!

Tools & Supplies

- ◎ Half-gallon (2-L) milk carton
- ◎ Chopstick or pencil
- ◎ 15-inch (37.5-cm) length of thick thread
- ◎ Metal nut
- ◎ Plastic drinking straw
- ◎ Paper clip
- ◎ Index card
- ◎ Scissors
- ◎ Tape
- ◎ Colored paper
- ◎ Markers
- ◎ Glue
- ◎ Beans

HOLES HERE

Let's build it!

1. Poke holes through the top of a milk carton. Force a chopstick or pencil through the holes so that one end juts out like an arm.

2. String the thread through the nut, then through a 5-inch (12.5-cm) section of the drinking straw as shown. Tie it to a paper clip.

3. Draw a flying superhero on an index card. Cut it out and tape it to the straw.

4. Cut out a piece of blue paper to fit the side of the milk carton. Use markers and paper cutouts to make a sky scene. Glue the decorated paper panel to the front of the milk carton beneath the arm. This is the backdrop for your superhero's flight.

5. Fill the milk carton with just enough beans to hold it steady.

6. Hook the paper clip onto the arm and set your hero swinging back and forth!

A *pendulum* is simply a weight hanging from a string.

Back & Forth

Fast Physics

Swing High, Swing Low

Pendulums are everywhere: hanging lamps, dangling earrings — there's even one at the playground. That's right, a swing is a pendulum!

Have a friend pull you back in a swing and then release you. What happens if you don't pump? Gravity pulls you down and the force of friction gradually slows the swinging motion. Your swing will eventually come to a stop right where it started: directly below the structure it hangs from.

Pump hard, then stop. Can you feel yourself swinging faster as you approach the ground and slowing as you rise?

How'd That Happen?

The swing and the Pendulum Pal are powered by you and gravity! Pull the weight to the side, and you give it stored (potential) energy. Release the weight and it falls, and the pull of gravity changes stored energy to moving (kinetic) energy. The pendulum rises to about the same position on the other side. This swinging action would go on forever if it weren't for the slowing force of friction (page 28), which makes each swing a little lower than the last.

!? Excited by the change from kinetic to potential energy and back again? You bet! That's how a roller coaster ride works. Kinetic energy is maxed when the car reaches its greatest speed. And potential energy is maxed when the car is at its highest point. How thrilling!

GALILEO GALILEI

Open Eyes, Open Mind

In 1583, Galileo Galilei (yup, the same brilliant scientist mentioned on page 54) made an earthshaking observation that most of us would never have noticed. While sitting in church, as the story goes, Galileo noticed a hanging lamp swinging back and forth. Although each arc (swing) was shorter than the last, each seemed to take the same length of time. Was it true, he questioned?

An accurate timing device did not yet exist, so resourceful Galileo tested his hunch by measuring the swings against his pulse. He was right! Galileo's principle of the pendulum marked the beginning of the science of dynamics (force and motion) as we understand it today.

!? Imagine one single, super source for most energy on Earth! Well, guess what? You're imagining the sun. Most energy comes from the sun. The sun's rays provide the energy for plants to grow. You eat plants (like carrots) or food that comes from animals eating plants (like burgers). This energy gives you muscle power to lift a pendulum and power a gizmo. So, strange as it seems, the sun helps power Pendulum Pal and Bob Dog ... and you!

BOB DOG

This dog's head works like a pendulum. The modeling clay is the weight; the cup acts like the string. Push the head and you store energy in the weight! Gravity pulls the cup downward with enough force to move the weight to the other side. Then, the cup swings back up again, flipping the weight back again. Back and forth, until the head comes to rest. Arf!

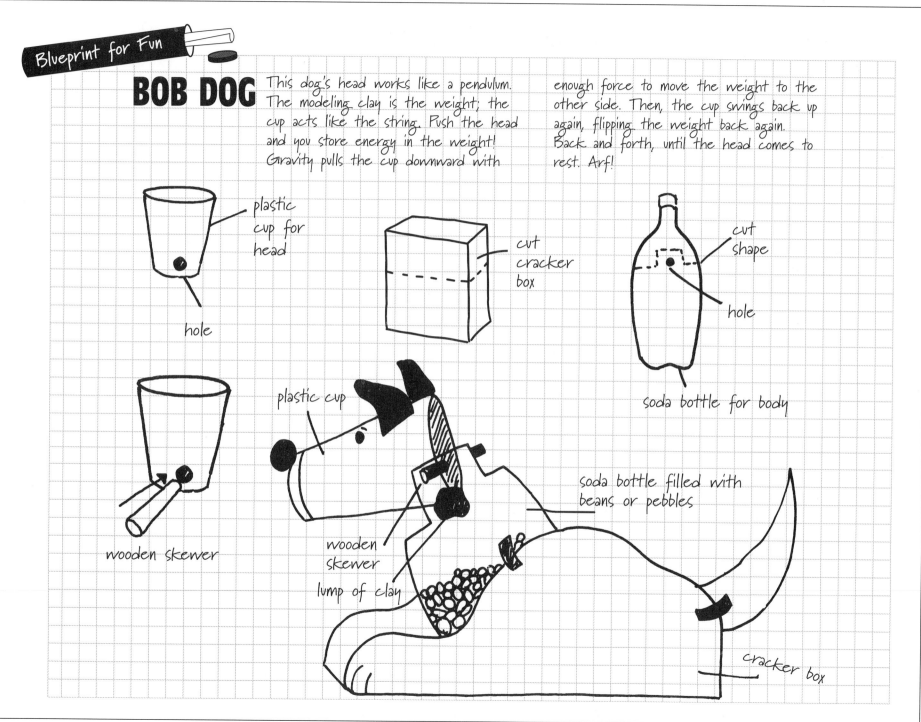

plastic cup for head

hole

cut cracker box

cut shape

hole

soda bottle for body

plastic cup

soda bottle filled with beans or pebbles

wooden skewer

wooden skewer

lump of clay

cracker box

Knock It Off!

Can you move a marble without touching it? Rig up this contraption to find out!

Tools & Supplies
- ◎ Cardboard egg carton
- ◎ Scissors
- ◎ Tape
- ◎ Marbles (all the same size)
- ◎ Lid

Let's build it!

1. Cut these sections from an egg carton.

2. Set up the sections and tape the troughs together.

3. Set a chain of five marbles in the level trough section. Be sure they are touching one another.

Cut from the bottom

Cut from the lid

Cut from long edges of lid

- ◎ Roll one marble down the ramp.
- ◎ Roll two marbles down the ramp.
- ◎ Experiment with different numbers of rollers and marbles in the chain.
- ◎ Try spacing the marbles in the chain an inch (2.5 cm) apart.

What happens when rollers collide with the chain of marbles? One marble is hit first, but which and how many roll away?

HIT & RUN

The rolling marble is moving, so it has energy of motion (the kinetic kind). It hits the first marble in the chain, but the last marble rolls away. The moving marble's energy is transferred through the entire chain! Two moving marbles have twice as much energy as one marble, so they knock two marbles off the chain. Amazing!

CRASH!

YAY!

You Can't Create It ... You Can't Destroy It ... Energy Rules!

Energy can be changed from one form to another, but **the total amount of energy never changes.** One marble colliding with a marble chain causes only one marble at the end of the chain to scoot away. Scientists call this *conservation of energy*. **Energy can not be created or destroyed, only transferred or changed.**

!? What causes a wave to get 10 times taller than you? Earthquakes under the ocean make tidal waves, or *tsunamis*. Out at sea, you might float over one and not even notice it. But when they come to shore, look out. With the same amount of energy they had out at sea but with far less water to push on, gigantic waves crash on the beach!

Coin Combo

Place a penny about half an inch (1 cm) away from a nickel on one side, and place another penny right up against the nickel on the other. Hold the nickel in place with your finger. Use a finger from your other hand to shoot the free penny into the nickel. What happens to the other penny? Try this with all sorts of coin combinations.

Follow the Bouncing Ball

Drop a Ping-Pong ball from about 2 feet (60 cm) above an empty bathtub. Now, drop it from the same height above your bed. Compare the bounces. Why the difference?

Answers: Coin combo. The other penny shoots away, just as in the marble chain. **Bouncing ball.** Over the tub's hard surface, much of the ball's energy went into the bounce. But over the bed, much of the ball's energy was spent pushing into the covers. It all adds up to the same amount of released energy!

AMAZING SWINGERS

This contraption makes a fascinating centerpiece. Challenge dinner guests to guess how it works! Hold one figure still while you start the other swinging. Then let go and watch how the energy is transferred from one figure to the other along the string!

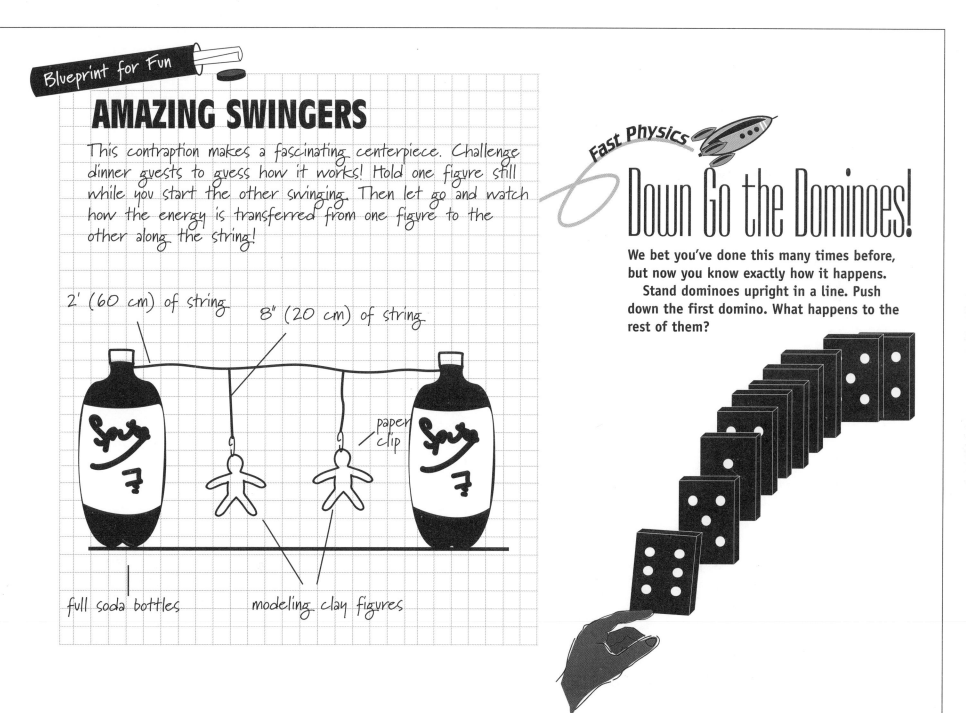

2' (60 cm) of string

8" (20 cm) of string

paper clip

full soda bottles

modeling clay figures

Fast Physics

Down Go the Dominoes!

We bet you've done this many times before, but now you know exactly how it happens.

Stand dominoes upright in a line. Push down the first domino. What happens to the rest of them?

Answer: *They fall, one by one! You push on the first one, and the energy is transferred down the line.*

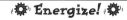

Pinwheel Power

Use the energy of moving air to help a clown perform!

Let's build it!

Make the pinwheel

1. Fold an 8½ x 8½ (21 cm x 21 cm) square piece of paper into a triangle shape two times. Unfold it and you will see an "X" shape. Cut a little over halfway down each crease. Tape every other point together, close to the tip.

2. Unbend a jumbo clip and poke it through the center of the pinwheel.

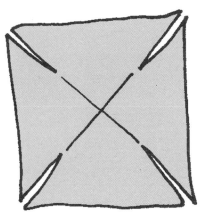

Build the windmill

1. Cover the face of the box with blue paper "sky." Glue on shapes for white clouds and a brown circus tent.

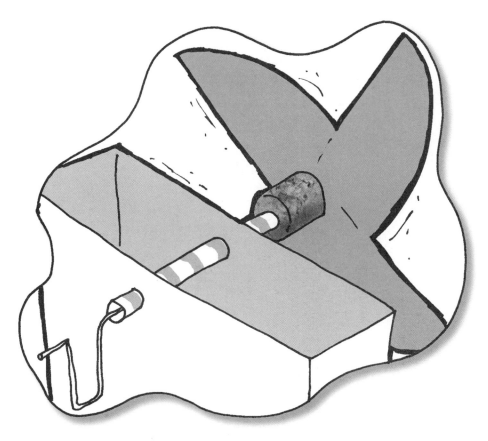

2. Punch holes in either side of the box and insert a section of drinking straw. Poke the wire shaft of the pinwheel through a cork and then through the straw.

3. Bend the wire into a "U" shape on the other side.

4. Cut out a clown from paper. Attach its arms and legs with thread. Poke its hands through the wire as shown.

5. Set the pinwheel in the breeze, or blow directly into it yourself. Watch the clown perform its antics!

Turn, Turn, Turn

How'd That Happen?

The pinwheel is a clever way to change the shape of paper so that it catches moving air. Moving air has energy that is transferred to the pinwheel. Air pushes into the sails and makes the pinwheel rotate around the center point. In other words, it spins!

Inventor's Workshop

Windy Whirlers

Put a pinwheel on your head, toss one in the air, and hang a few in the breeze! Then, invent your own way to use pinwheel power!

Every Which Way

1. Make three duo-color pinwheels from 5½-inch (13.5-cm) squares. Connect the tips to each other with tape. Do not connect them to the center.
2. Make four small pinwheels from 3-inch (7.5-cm) squares. Assemble them as shown with a long pin through the center.
3. Put them all together using plastic drinking straws, thin string or fishing line, and a couple of weights. Hang by an open window or on a porch.

Get A-Head

This action wear makes any other party hat seem boring!

It's a Toss-Up

Make a classic 6-inch (15-cm) pinwheel. Slip a small section of a plastic drinking straw onto the pin before sticking into the side of an eraser or cork. Toss high in the air or down a stairwell.

Create a Spectacular Spinner

- Color the paper first with markers.
- Cut the pinwheel from colorful wrapping paper, magazine pages, or foil.
- Cut two wheels from two different colors of paper at the same time and assemble as one sheet for a duo-color pinwheel.

Wind Wonder

A turning motion can make electricity. How do you get the most turning motion possible? Create super-efficient windmills, or wind turbines. Design the blades like airplane wings to produce the greatest speed. Set hundreds in an open, windy field. Bingo! You've got a wonderful wind farm producing lots of free, clean energy from the wind!

Whose Bright Idea?

THOMAS EDISON

SEE THE LIGHT

Sit for five minutes in the dark one night, and you'll be glad Thomas Edison didn't get discouraged with his experiments. By observing lightning, Edison knew electricity could glow. The problem was how to run electricity through a filament (fiber) without it burning up. Even though he placed the filament in a vacuum bulb (one with no air inside), the fiber still burned up. Edison tested more than 300 fibers in 1878, including a hair from his assistant's beard. All of them failed. When asked if he was ready to give up, he answered, "Not at all!" Now that he knew which 300 fibers *wouldn't* work, he figured he had made lots of progress!

The Inventor's Mind Says ...

No wonder Edison became such a famous inventor. He had the right frame of mind. Like all good inventors with a problem to solve, he asked himself: *What else could this be used for? How else could this be done? Is there another way I haven't thought of yet?* Then he tested his ideas, as many times as needed. Even when faced with failure, he didn't give up. Instead, he asked himself, *What did I learn from what didn't work?*

Putting It All Together

Congratulations! You are now an expert builder of gizmos and gadgets, and an authority on the laws of physics as well. Combine your favorite contraptions from this book with your creative thinking to make a super gizmo, your very own awesome invention. Have a problem that bugs you? *You* can solve it!

Index

More Good Books From Williamson Publishing

**Williamson books are available from your bookseller or directly from Williamson Publishing.
Please see last page for ordering information or to visit our Web site.**

More Williamson Books by Jill Hauser!

American Bookseller Pick of the Lists
Oppenheim Toy Portfolio Gold Seal Award
Benjamin Franklin Juvenile Nonfiction
 Book of the Year
Teachers' Choice Award
◎ **SUPER SCIENCE CONCOCTIONS**
50 Mysterious Mixtures for Fabulous Fun
Ages 6-12, 160 pages, $12.95

American Bookseller Pick of the Lists
Dr. Toy Best Vacation Product
◎ **KIDS' CRAZY ART CONCOCTIONS**
50 Mysterious Mixtures for Art & Craft Fun
Ages 6-12, 160 pages, $12.95

Early Childhood New Directors' Choice Award
Parents' Choice Approved
◎ **SCIENCE PLAY!**
Beginning Discoveries for 2- to 6-Year-Olds
Ages 2-6, 144 pages, $12.95

◎ **GROWING UP READING**
Learning to Read Through Creative Play
Ages 1-6, 144 pages, $12.95

 ## Williamson's
Kids Can!® Books ... Where all kids can soar!
The following *Kids Can!*® books for children ages 4 to 12 are each 144-178 pages, fully illustrated, trade paper, 11 x 8½, $12.95 US.

Benjamin Franklin Best Education/
 Teaching Book Award
Oppenheim Toy Portfolio Best Book Award
American Bookseller Pick of the Lists
◎ **THE KIDS' SCIENCE BOOK**
Creative Experiences for Hands-On Fun
by Robert Hirschfeld and Nancy White

Parent's Guide Children's Media Award
Teachers' Choice Award
Dr. Toy Best Vacation Product
◎ **CUT-PAPER PLAY!**
Dazzling Creations from Construction Paper
by Sandi Henry

Early Childhood News Directors' Choice Award
◎ **VROOM! VROOM!**
Making 'dozers, 'copters, trucks & more
by Judy Press

Parent's Guide Children's Media Award
Parents' Choice Approved
◎ **BOREDOM BUSTERS!**
The Curious Kids' Activity Book
by Avery Hart & Paul Mantell

Parent's Guide Children's Media Award
Parents' Choice Approved
◎ **MAKING COOL CRAFTS & AWESOME ART!**
A Kids' Treasure Trove of Fabulous Fun
by Roberta Gould

Parents' Choice Gold Award (Original edition)
Dr. Toy Best Vacation Product
◎ **THE KIDS' NATURE BOOK**
365 Indoor/Outdoor Activities and Experiences
by Susan Milord

Benjamin Franklin Best Multicultural Book Award
Parents' Choice Approved
Skipping Stones Multicultural Honor Award
◎ **THE KIDS' MULTICULTURAL COOKBOOK**
Food & Fun Around the World
by Deanna F. Cook

Parent's Guide Children's Media Award
Parents' Choice Approved
◎ **MAKING COOL CRAFTS & AWESOME ART!**
A Kids' Treasure Trove of Fabulous Fun
by Roberta Gould

Children's Book-of-the-Month Club Selection
◎ **KIDS' COMPUTER CREATIONS**
Using Your Computer for Art & Craft Fun
by Carol Sabbeth

Parents' Choice Approved
Dr. Toy Best Vacation Product
◎ **KIDS GARDEN!**
The Anytime, Anyplace Guide to Sowing & Growing Fun
by Avery Hart and Paul Mantell

Parents' Choice Gold Award
American Bookseller Pick of the Lists
Oppenheim Toy Portfolio Best Book Award
◎ **THE KIDS' MULTICULTURAL ART BOOK**
Art & Craft Experiences from Around the World
by Alexandra M. Terzian

Parents' Choice Gold Award
Benjamin Franklin Best Juvenile Nonfiction Award
◎ **KIDS MAKE MUSIC!**
Clapping and Tapping from Bach to Rock
by Avery Hart and Paul Mantell

American Bookseller Pick of the Lists
Oppenheim Toy Portfolio Best Book Award
Skipping Stones Nature & Ecology Honor Award
◎ **EcoArt!**
Earth-Friendly Art & Craft Experiences for 3- to 9-Year-Olds
by Laurie Carlson

Selection of Book-of-the-Month; Scholastic Book Clubs
◎ **KIDS COOK!**
Fabulous Food for the Whole Family
by Sarah Williamson and Zachary Williamson

◎ **THE KIDS' WILDLIFE BOOK**
Exploring Animal Worlds through Indoor/Outdoor Crafts & Experiences
by Warner Shedd

◎ **HANDS AROUND THE WORLD**
365 Creative Ways to Build Cultural Awareness & Global Respect
by Susan Milord

Parents' Choice Approved
◎ **KIDS CREATE!**
Art & Craft Experiences for 3- to 9-Year-Olds
by Laurie Carlson

Parents Magazine Parents' Pick
◎ **KIDS LEARN AMERICA!**
Bringing Geography to Life with People, Places, & History
by Patricia Gordon and Reed C. Snow

Parents' Choice Recommended
American Bookseller Pick of the Lists
◎ **ADVENTURES IN ART**
Art & Craft Experiences for 8- to 13-Year-Olds
by Susan Milord

Parent's Guide Children's Media Award
Benjamin Franklin Best Education/ Teaching Book Award
◎ **HAND-PRINT ANIMAL ART**
by Carolyn Carreiro
full color, $14.95

◎ **SUMMER FUN!**
60 Activities for a Kid-Perfect Summer
by Susan Williamson

◎ **KIDS' ART WORKS!**
Creating with Color, Design, Texture & More
by Sandi Henry

◎ **THE KIDS' BOOK OF NATURAL HISTORY ACTIVITIES**
Dinos, Fossils, Biomes & More
by Judy Press

Williamson's
Kaleidoscope Kids™
Books ... *Where learning meets life!*

Kaleidoscope Kids™ books allow children ages 6 to 12 to explore a subject from many different angles, using many different skills. All books are 96 pages, two-color, fully illustrated, 10 x 10, $10.95 US.

Children's Book Council Notable Book
American Bookseller Pick of the Lists
Dr. Toy 10 Best Educational Products
◎ **PYRAMIDS!**
50 Hands-On Activities to Experience Ancient Egypt
by Avery Hart & Paul Mantell

Parent's Guide Children's Media Award
American Bookseller Pick of the Lists
Dr. Toy 100 Best Children's Products
◎ **KNIGHTS & CASTLES**
50 Hands-On Activities to Experience the Middle Ages
by Avery Hart & Paul Mantell

◎ **ANCIENT GREECE!**
40 Hands-On Activities to Experience This Wondrous Age
by Avery Hart and Paul Mantell

American Bookseller Pick of the Lists
◎ **MEXICO!**
40 Activities to Experience Mexico Past and Present
by Susan Milord

◎ **BRIDGES!**
Amazing Structures to Design, Build & Test
by Carol Johmann and Elizabeth Rieth

◎ **GEOLOGY ROCKS!**
50 Hands-On Activities to Explore the Earth
by Cindy Blobaum

◎ **THE BEAST IN YOU!**
Activities & Questions to Explore Evolution
by Marc McCutcheon

Williamson's
Tales Alive!® Books ...
A feast of folklore fun for ages 4 and up!

These beautiful, full-color books focus on retellings of multicultural folktales accompanied by original paintings and activities to round out a child's understanding of a tale and its subject. Books are 96-128 pages, full-color, 8½ x 11.

Benjamin Franklin Best Juvenile Fiction
Parents' Choice Honor Award
Skipping Stones Multicultural Honor Award
◎ **TALES ALIVE!**
Ten Multicultural Folktales with Activities
by Susan Milord
Trade paper, $15.95

Benjamin Franklin Best Juvenile Fiction
Benjamin Franklin Best Multicultural Book Award
Parents' Choice Approved
Teachers' Choice Award
◎ **TALES OF THE SHIMMERING SKY**
Ten Global Folktales with Activities
by Susan Milord
Trade paper, $15.95

Storytelling World Honor Award
◎ **Tales Alive!**
BIRD TALES from Near and Far
by Susan Milord
Trade paper, $14.95

Williamson's
Little Hands® Books ...
Setting the stage for learning

The following *Little Hands*® books for children ages 2 to 6 are each 144 pages, fully illustrated, trade paper, 10 x 8, $12.95 US.

Parent's Guide Children's Media Award
◎ **ALPHABET ART**
With A to Z Animal Art & Fingerplays
by Judy Press

American Bookseller Pick of the Lists
◎ **RAINY DAY PLAY!**
Explore, Create, Discover, Pretend
by Nancy Fusco Castaldo

Parents' Choice Gold Award
Children's Book-of-the-Month Club Selection
◎ **FUN WITH MY 5 SENSES**
Activities to Build Learning Readiness
by Sarah A. Williamson

Children's Book-of-the-Month Club Main Selection
◎ **THE LITTLE HANDS ART BOOK**
Exploring Arts & Crafts with 2- to 6-Year-Olds
by Judy Press

Parents' Choice Approved
Early Childhood News Directors' Choice Award
◎ **SHAPES, SIZES & MORE SURPRISES!**
A Little Hands Early Learning Book
by Mary Tomczyk

Parents' Choice Approved
◎ **The Little Hands**
BIG FUN CRAFT BOOK
Creative Fun for 2- to 6-Year-Olds
by Judy Press

Parents' Choice Approved
◉ **THE LITTLE HANDS NATURE BOOK**
Earth, Sky, Critters & More
by Nancy Fusco Castaldo

◉ **MATH PLAY!**
80 Ways to Count & Learn
by Diane McGowan and Mark Schrooten

Williamson's
Good Times™ Books

Skipping Stones Ecology and Nature Award
Parents' Choice Approved
The National Parenting Center Seal of Approval
◉ **MONARCH MAGIC!**
Butterfly Activities & Nature Discoveries
by Lynn M. Rosenblatt
Ages 4-12, 96 pages, more than 100 full-color
photos, 8 x 10, $12.95

Parents' Choice Approved
◉ **KIDS' PUMPKIN PROJECTS**
Planting & Harvest Fun
by Deanna F. Cook
Ages 4-10, 96 pages, fully illustrated,
8 x 10, $8.95

Visit Our Web Site!

To see what's new at Williamson and learn more
about specific books, visit our Web site at:
http://www.williamsonbooks.com

· ·

To Order Books:

You'll find Williamson books at your favorite bookstore, or order directly form
Williamson Publishing. We accept Visa and MasterCard *(please indicate the number
and expiration date)*, or send check to:

Williamson Publishing Company
Church Hill Road, P.O. Box 185
Charlotte, Vermont 05445

Toll-free phone orders with credit cards:

1-800-234-8791

E-mail orders with credit cards: **order@williamsonbooks.com**
Catalog request: **mail, phone, or e-mail**

Please add **$3.20** for postage for one book plus **50 cents** for each additional book.
Satisfaction is guaranteed or full refund without questions or quibbles.

Prices may be slightly higher when purchased in Canada.

Kids Can!®, *Little Hands*®, and *Tales Alive!*® are registered trademarks of Williamson
Publishing. *Kaleidoscope Kids*™ and *Good Times*™ are
trademarks of Williamson Publishing.